Cumbria Library Services

COUNTY COUNCIL

This book is due for return on or before the last date above.
It may be renewed by personal application, post or telephone,
if not in demand.

C.L. 18F

post or telephone, if not in demand.

C.L.18

THE CUILLIN

The edge of man's spirit will be ground
on the bare sharp summits of mountains
SORLEY MACLEAN, 'The Cuillin'

THE CUILLIN

GREAT MOUNTAIN RIDGE OF SKYE

GORDON STAINFORTH

CONSTABLE
LONDON

FIRST PUBLISHED IN GREAT BRITAIN 1994
BY CONSTABLE AND COMPANY LIMITED
3 THE LANCHESTERS, 162 FULHAM PALACE ROAD
LONDON W6 9ER

ISBN 0 09 471550 5

PRINTED IN HONG KONG BY
WORLD PRINT LTD

A CIP CATALOGUE RECORD FOR THIS BOOK
IS AVAILABLE FROM THE BRITISH LIBRARY

HALF-TITLE:
The Cuillin from near Elgol
TITLE:
The Cuillin from Sron Daraich,
near Tokavaig, in early March
CONTENTS:
The central part of the Cuillin main ridge
in winter, from Sgurr Beag

CONTENTS

1
FIRST IMPRESSIONS
PAGE 17

2
THE BRITISH ALPS
PAGE 57

3
A WAY OF LIFE
PAGE 107

4
THE GREAT TRAVERSE
PAGE 123

MAP
PAGE 156

THE CUILLIN SUMMITS
PAGE 158

THE CUILLIN MAIN RIDGE
PAGE 162

PHOTOGRAPHIC NOTES
PAGE 170

BIBLIOGRAPHY
PAGE 174

ACKNOWLEDGEMENTS
PAGE 175

INDEX
PAGE 176

Far, far distant, far on a horizon,
I see the rocking of the antlered Cuillin,
beyond the seas of sorrow, beyond the morass of agony,
I see the white felicity of the high-towered mountains.

SORLEY MACLEAN

The Cuillin in January, from near
Drynoch

Sgurr nan Gillean and Bruach na
Frithe from near Drynoch

The Cuillin seen from the northern
end of Loch Harport in September
and, overleaf, from Sgiath-bheinn
Tokavaig in May

The prospect to the west was that of desolation itself; a savage series of rude mountains, discoloured, black and red, as if by the rage of fire. The serrated tops of Blaven affect with astonishment: and beyond them, the clustered height of Quillin . . .

THOMAS PENNANT 1772

Here and there a black precipitous scaur looms out of the hillside, but the hills themselves in their white dresses are folded softly against the sky, and the snowy peaks of the Coolins shimmer away like some ethereal phantasy into the sapphire heaven. Were it not for the shadows cast on the hills by their outstanding rocks and bluffs, they might be fleecy clouds, forming and dispersing and reforming in the dreamy air.

J.A.MACCULOCH, 1908

The northern end of the Main Ridge above Glen Drynoch on a cold evening in March

Page 12/13:
The Cuillin Main Ridge from the summit of Beinn Dearg Mhor at dusk

1

FIRST IMPRESSIONS

The Main Ridge above Glen Drynoch
on a stormy evening in February

The great blue mass of the Cuillin with profile so clean cut and memorable as a historical face was photographed in my mind before the days of Daguerre and Talbot, and the picture grows not dimmer but more distinct with each year.

ALEXANDER NICOLSON

THE PROMISED LAND

When first seen by the traveller on the distant horizon, the great mountain ridge of the Cuillin is one of the most evocative sights in Britain. It stands on the skyline like a massive castellated fortress, strangely reassuring in its clear-cut solidity, yet wrapped in a haze of mystery. It is a fantasy, a mountain lover's dream, a vision full of indefinite hopes and climbing possibilities. For Lawrence Pilkington, one of the first pioneers here in the last century, it was, as for so many since, 'a glimpse of the Promised Land'.

The peaks that make up the Cuillin may not have the sheer scale and grandeur of the Alps, but they have nevertheless a grandeur and atmosphere all of their own. Rising more or less straight out of the sea to a height of over three thousand feet, they share something of the character of both the high mountains and the Atlantic seaboard.

Experts are now generally agreed that the name 'Cuillin' derives from the Norse word 'kjölen' which denotes not only a high mountain ridge but also the keel of a boat. It is entirely appropriate that the Viking mariners should have given such a simple, singular name to such a distinctive landmark which does indeed vaguely resemble a long ship. (A prominent transverse ridge is actually called Druim nam Ramh, the 'Ridge of Oars'.) It also no doubt reminded them of their own Kjölen, or high mountain region, back home in Norway. The similarity in pronunciation to the Gaelic word 'cuilionn', meaning 'holly', is fortuitous; the prickly distant outline of the Ridge certainly has something of the holly leaf about it, which is probably why this derivation found favour among etymologists in the last century. The correct Gaelic spelling should in fact be An Cuilfhionn, An Cuilithionn or An Culthionn.

Left:
The Cuillin from Tokavaig bay in March

The northern end of the ridge from Coire Riabhach

Irrespective of its derivation, the plural, Anglicized form of the name, 'the Cuillins', is as incorrect as calling the Caucasus 'the Caucasuses' or the Himalaya 'the Himalayas', and only slightly less grating to the enthusiast's ear than the cringe-making 'Cuillin Hills' – which makes them sound like something akin to the Cotswolds. The originator of this travesty should have been swung on the end of a long rope from one of the many high and very *un*-hill-like points that are to be found on the Main Ridge.

Whether the collective name of the Cuillin should be treated as singular or plural is something of a moot point. It depends very much on the context: as individual peaks, the Cuillin *are* no less impressive than the Cuillin *is* when regarded from a distance as one great mountain ridge. Generally, I prefer to think of the whole range collectively, as one singular phenomenon.

This is rather more than a linguistic quibble for, geologically, the Cuillin is much less a collection of individual peaks than one great mountain massif formed by a gigantic 'pluton', or intrusion of igneous rock from deep below the earth's crust. This is no ordinary orogenic phenomenon – a mountain mass formed by the folding or buckling of the earth's crust – but something altogether more infernal, caused by a cataclysmic rupturing of the crust that allowed the magma, the molten layer beneath the earth's crust, to well up from the depths like a gigantic carbuncle. The Cuillin Pluton is a geological anomaly of enormous proportions, and it has given rise to a freak landscape which has nothing in common with the surrounding, pre-existing rocks, nor for that matter, with anything else in Britain (apart from the smaller, neighbouring Cuillin of Rum.) It is entirely 'other', a gargantuan land form of singular power and might.

When one speaks of the 'power' of the Cuillin landscape, one is not, for once, using a tired old metaphor, because here it is true. The colossal forces and temperatures which were involved in forcing billions of cubic feet of molten magma up into a mighty dome or 'batholith' several miles thick defies the imagination. The batholith or pluton was, in effect, an enormous reservoir of magma, feeding a vast system of volcanoes (long since eroded away) which originally extended above it for over ten thousand feet. The upward pressure continued even as the gabbro rock was solidifying, so that it became seamed by a multitude of fissures through which further molten rock was forced from below. Today, all we are looking at are the highly eroded remnants of the solidified magma reservoir.

It is not until we see the Cuillin at close quarters that we can fully appreciate its power. It is altogether more extreme in character than is apparent from a distance. The contrast, for example, between the rather benign appearance of Sgurr nan

Sgurr nan Gillean towers above the Bhasteir Gorge

Gillean from Sligachan and the titanic saw-toothed reality that towers above the entrance to Coire Bhasteir has to be seen to be believed. Its sheer scale and precipitousness exceeds all expectations. And in every corrie it is the same story: we enter a truly Plutonian landscape of monstrous proportions.

Perhaps the most striking quality of the Cuillin is just how fresh and raw it looks, as if it was the work of a few nightmarish hours or days. In fact, the main intrusion was a protracted process lasting five million years or more, starting about seventy million years ago, with further major periods of volcanic activity sixty and fifty-five million years ago. Just how recent this is in geological terms becomes clear when we realize that these mountains had not even begun to be formed until *after* the age of the dinosaurs, and even then there was a long period of erosion in which all the overlying volcanic rock was removed before the onset of the Ice Age about six hundred thousand years ago. The Ice Age was largely responsible for producing the landscape of narrow ridges and deep corries that we know today, while the serrated, pinnacled crest is mainly the result of the varying resistance to erosion of the rock, the massive gabbro being seamed by more fissile basalt dykes.

The bottom of the Pinnacle Ridge of
Sgurr nan Gillean seen in profile from
Meall Odhar

Right:
The mighty precipice of Sron na
Ciche reflected in Loch Lagan on a
May evening

Compared with the giant Son of Cuillin
neither Goll nor Fionn nor monster
devised by man's imagination
was more than a louse on a beetle's back
compared with Cuchulain in his war gear.
What likeness knee or calf,
chest, thigh or mortal shoulder
to the ramparts of grim precipices
black with ice or with cold wet ooze,
to the heaving chest of the high mountain bluffs
surging in proud crags
like the mother-breasts of the world
erect with the universe's concupiscence.

SORLEY MACLEAN, 1939

The Great Prow of Blaven

Page 26:
The Great Stone Shoot of Sgurr
Alasdair from Sgurr Dearg

Page 27:
Coire Lagan and Sgurr Dearg from
the head of the Great Stone Shoot

24

Sgurr Eadar da Choire, Coire a'
Ghreadaidh

THE WASTELAND

Though the atmosphere, the weather and the light frequently
bestow beauty on it, the Cuillin Ridge, in itself, is emphatically not
a thing of beauty. Indeed there is much about it that is ugly and
crude. Overall, the impression is one of savage desolation. It has
such an alien, primeval quality that it might well be on another
planet. It is everything that is not normal.

For historical reasons, I am deliberately avoiding painting the
landscape in too romantic a light. One of the suggested
derivations of the name 'Cuillin' that I have avoided mentioning
so far is related to the Old Welsh Celtic word 'Coolin', meaning
'worthless' – a wasteland. The description of the landscape as a
'waste' has a sad and ironic ring of truth about it, for much of the
landscape is *unnaturally* wild, and much of the surrounding
desolation is the result of a tragedy which many people would
rather forget.

Lonely Harta Corrie from the
summit of Marsco

I am referring, of course, to the Clearances, mention of which cannot be avoided when talking about the Skye landscape – though sometimes this terrible era is glossed over and the story leaps straight from the ever-popular melodrama of Bonnie Prince Charlie's escape in 1746 to the arrival of the first heroic tourists in the early nineteenth century. The Clearances were the result of an enormous new demand for Scottish wool after about 1750; this, combined with the decline of the kelp industry, led to the forcible eviction of some 34,000 local crofters, who were deported to Canada and Australia to make way for the sheep. The landlords were helped in this by a curious local 'charity' called the Skye Emigration Society, which had government and Treasury backing.

A typical Writ of Removal in 1830 was worded:

> To all the crofters in Lorgill. Take notice that you are hereby duly warned that you all be ready to leave Lorgill at twelve o'clock on 4th August next with all your baggage but no stock and proceed to Loch Snizort, where you will board the ship *Midlothian* that will take you to Nova-Scotia where you are to receive a free grant of land from Her Majesty's Government. Take further notice that any crofter disobeying this order will be immediately arrested and taken to prison . . . This order is final and no appeal to the Government will be considered. God Save the Queen.

A crofter reflected at the time: 'There was neither sin nor sorrow in the world for us, but the clearances came upon us, destroying all, turning our gladness into bitterness, our blessings into blasphemy, and our Christianity into mockery.'

When Gladstone, in 1882, finally appointed a Royal Commission to look into this human tragedy, Lord Napier reported that he found 'a state of misery, of wrong-doing, and of patient long-suffering, without parallel in the history of our country.' It is indeed a sorry tale of inhumanity that lends a certain poignancy to the name 'Coolin'. Today the silent munching of the sheep around the ruined villages of Suisnish and Boreraig only serves to emphasize the absence of their long departed inhabitants.

Another dark side of the history of these mountains is the bloody and bloody-minded saga of the clan warfare between the Macleods and the Macdonalds. Perhaps the most notorious massacre was that which took place in the lonely Harta Corrie directly below the Cuillin Ridge. After a battle which lasted all day the Macleods were driven back to a defensive position beside the enormous boulder now known as the 'Bloody Stone', where they were all slaughtered. The bodies were piled up round the

The Bloody Stone, Harta Corrie

boulder; and legend has it that fairies made bows and arrows from the bones.

The last great feud between these unneighbourly clans was the so-called 'War of the One-Eyed Woman', which was apparently provoked by a Macdonald rejecting a Macleod's hand in marriage after a year-long engagement. (The defective eye was, it seems, a euphemism for a number of complaints.) The increasingly violent tit-for-tat which followed culminated, in 1601, in the very bloody Battle of Coire na Creiche (the 'Corrie of the Spoils'), again, right in the heart of the Main Cuillin. After this there was never an angry word again between them, or so we are told.

We have to guard against talking about these 'distant' horrors condescendingly, as if we have improved in our own barbaric century; and particularly against thinking that none of this harsh and tragic history can possibly be of any relevance to us now, or to our understanding of the landscape.

Coire na Creiche in early March

A LANDSCAPE OF EXTREMES

The Cuillin landscape is a place of extremes – not just a place of excess, but one of contrasts: hard, solid boulders are situated in soft and treacherous bogs; rough, reassuring gabbro is seamed with smooth, shattered basalt: the very sound and the very loose, the sure and the unreliable, the safe and the slippery, the stable and the precarious, the barren and the fruitful. Yes, fruitful: for among the harsh jumble of jagged rocks is to be found a myriad of exquisite mountain flowers – delicate, totally unexpected, almost absurdly ill-fitted to their surroundings. Out of the rock comes life; 'out of the strong came forth sweetness'. Minute Alpine flowers – beautiful, precious, defenceless – living in fragile harmony with the unrefined power and barbarity of this harsh landscape.

Sea campion (*Silene maritima*) on Sron Dearg screes

Roseroot *(Rhodiola rosea)* growing on a peridotite boulder, Caisteal a' Garbh-choire

Ptarmigan in Coir' a' Ghrunnda

But the rock is, in its own way, very beautiful and full of variety. The first great distinction is between the dark gabbro of the 'Black Cuillin' and the lighter coloured granite of the 'Red Cuillin'. These names were the invention of geologists at the end of the last century, apparently suggested by the local name for what is now the Red Cuillin, Na Beinnean Dearga, and they are highly misleading. The granite of the Red Cuillin is actually a pale straw colour, while the gabbro of the Black Cuillin is simply a darker brown. Only when it is wet and overcast does it appear at all black, and on a fine evening it is this rock rather than the granite that is likely to appear red. (For this reason I shall not be using the term Black Cuillin again in this book.) There are literally dozens of varieties of the gabbro, ranging all the way from the extraordinarily rough and spiky light, yellow-orange peridotite of Sgurr Dubh na Da Bheinn, to the immaculate, compact brown rock of the Cioch Buttress of Sron na Ciche – which is called *White Allivalite* by the geologists. Their sense of colour was obviously not equal to their petrological skills.

Right:
Sgurr Mhic Coinnich, Sgurr Alasdair and Sgurr Sgumain on a spring afternoon

Right, below:
Sgurr Mhic Coinnich rears above the slabs of upper Coire Lagan

Midsummer sunset on Am Basteir and the Basteir Tooth

Conceive these mountains if you can — rib them with gleaming waterfalls, paint them with ever changing hues and fill the intervening spaces with gorges, ravines and glens, dashed with the purple gloom and abysses illed with steaming mists, and you have some idea of the wondrous Cuillin.

C.R.WELD, 1859

Peridotite boulders in frozen Loch Coir' a' Ghrunnda, in March

Right:
Loch Lagan in May

Oxide stains on the side of Allt Coir' a' Mhadaidh

Looking out towards Rum from Beinn Dearg Mhor in the late evening

The fact that the Cuillin is not always black and sombre, but often a place of colour, is reflected in some of the mountain names: Sgurr a'Fionn Choire, Sgurr Dubh, Sgurr Dearg, Clach Glas, Bla Bheinn – white, black, red, grey, blue. Add to this the extreme contrasts provided by the weather – cloud and sun, sun and rain, rain and storm, storm and lightning, mist and sunshine, sunshine and hail, hail and wind, wind and calm, heat waves and ice, snow and sleet, sunbeams and rainbows, thunderbolts and Brocken Spectres – and it becomes clear that this is not a place one can generalize about at all easily.

Coire Lagan and Loch Brittle revealed through clearing cloud on Sgurr Mhic Coinnich

Rainbow and Glamaig on a stormy
day in February

Page 40:
On Ruadh Stac in February: Loch na
Creitheach and Loch Scavaig seen
through spindrift

Page 41:
A few minutes later

Loch an Athain and Srath na
Creitheach from the summit of Blaven,
in July

The heaven-kissing peaks of this strange group never fail to attract a portion of the vapours, which rising from the Atlantic, are constantly floating eastward to water the continent of Europe; and fancy is kept on the stretch, to find resemblances for the quick succession of fantastic appearances which the spirits of the air are working on the weather-beaten brow of these hills of song.

G. ANDERSON, 1834

The view east from Bealach Coire Lagan in May: cloud rolling towards Blaven

Wispy cloud on Druim Hain, seen from the summit of Ruadh Stac

Sgurr Dubh Beag and An Garbh-choire
on a moody morning in Coir'-uisg

Right:
Gars-bheinn and Loch Coruisk

All that can be said about the Cuillin weather is that it is extraordinarily fickle, a defier of all forecasts. Often, when it seems least likely, a day turns out much *better* than was forecast. Disgruntled tourists tend to exaggerate how bad the weather can be. My experience is that it is extremely rare for the Cuillin to be in the cloud for more than four days in a row. Usually it is much less. During the 150 days that I was on location taking the photographs for this book, the Main Ridge was completely clear of the cloud on 71 days. And this included a summer which was regarded as unusually bad even by the locals.

Those who are familiar with the Cuillin weather will be amused by Charles Pilkington's opinion on the subject in the 1880s:

> My personal experience of Skye weather is that it is the driest place in the British Isles, for I have been there three times, spending at least ten days on each occasion, and have only had four hours' rain in the three visits.

But he goes on to admit that it can be

> 'a wee bit moist' sometimes, as Walker, Hulton, and my brother Lawrence found to their cost in the autumn of 1883. My brother writes of this expedition, 'For three weeks it rained more or less every day: when the barometer fell it rained cats and dogs; when the barometer rose a sea mist crept up the hills in the morning, and turning into persistent rain did not clear off until the evening. Indeed it was only by getting up determinedly at 5 a.m. whenever the glass showed signs of rising, and walking sometimes eight or ten miles to the foot of our peak, and then waiting hours for a break in the weather, that we were able to make any ascents at all.'

Although long periods of bad weather here seem interminable, the rewards when it is fine are such that all the wasted days are quickly forgotten. Any Cuillin enthusiast will tell you the same: here you have to take the rough with the smooth. And what better spokesman than the great pioneer, Alexander Nicolson, who made the first ascent of Sgurr Alasdair in 1873?

> Nor let them imagine that they are all ill-used martyrs if they come for three days and the heavens refuse to show one morsel of blue – if they can't afford to wait for a fair blink the more's the pity for themselves. If they are in a hurry, Skye and its clouds (and its inhabitants) are in none, and the Cuillin will unveil their majestic heads, in due time and no sooner.

The north ridge of Clach Glas looms through the mist

Perhaps though the clouds towards the evening may break, then the torn masses of vapour, tearing in mad hunt along the ridges, will be lit up by the rays of the sun slowly descending into the western sea, and as the light flashes from the black rocks, and the shadows deepen in the corries, the superb beauty, the melancholy, the mystery of these mountains of the Isle of Mist will be revealed.

PROF NORMAN COLLIE, 1897

Clach Glas and Blaven emerge from the cloud

Right:
Am Basteir from the West Ridge of Sgurr nan Gillean

En route to the heart of the Cuillin: the head of Loch Scavaig

THE LURE OF THE WILD

What is it about the Cuillin that attracts people despite the weather? It seems that for most pilgrims (and that is not too strong a word) they have much more than a simple aesthetic appeal. To a greater extent perhaps than any other wild mountains in Britain, they have a very seductive quality. They stand there for all time on the horizon, compelling, enticing, luring us on. What the first great conservationist, John Muir, said of the Sierra Nevada in California is apposite here: 'The charms of these mountains are beyond all common reason, unexplainable and mysterious as life itself.' Perhaps the climber's fascination with them is simply a fundamental curiosity about the raw

The author crossing the Bad Step on the coastal path to Loch Coruisk

natural world and how we relate to it at the most basic level. That is, we want to learn how, if at all, we 'fit' into the natural world in its unspoilt state. Can we really get close to it in any meaningful sense? Can we really, as it were, 'hook' onto it with our boots and fingertips? Or are we merely *pretending* something – kidding ourselves, and others, that we are very tough and natural in every sense; that we are an élite who are 'returning to nature'?

Certainly, in a landscape such as this we get closer to our real selves. Here, stripped of our masks and pretences, we come face to face with our limitations and our inadequacies. The experience is not only sobering, but refreshing: here we really can recharge our batteries. But our motive for being here must be more than this. It's not just ourselves that we're interested in, but that missing link with the natural world. It is as if this primitive, almost sterile setting holds, in some strange way, the key to life itself, some vital secret. Although it makes us feel very small and insignificant, how significant it seems to us! It is redolent, not just of geological forces beyond our comprehension, but of something altogether less tangible. It seems somehow to be pregnant with an inner creative power that has a crucial relevance to our lives, even if we cannot say exactly what it is.

Right:
Loch Coruisk at dusk

Late evening: the River Scavaig
cascades into the sea

Loch Coruisk at dawn

So suddenly and unexpectedly does this strange scene break on the view, so unlike it is to the sea bay without, so dissimilar to all other scenery, and so little to be foreseen in a narrow insulated spot like Sky, that I felt as if transported by some magician into the enchanted wilds of an Arabian tale, carried to the habitations of Genii among the mysterious recesses of Caucasus.

JOHN MACCULOCH, 1819

2

THE BRITISH ALPS

Spring snow on Bruach na Frithe, Sgurr a'
Fionn Choire and Am Basteir

*Now, turning to the north, and
sweeping the horizon from east to
west, what do we see? Peaks and
pinnacles, jagged crests and
fantastic outlines; a wilderness of
weird shapes, dark, solemn, and
awful. Giant Sgor-na-Gillean is
there, the monarch of the
Cuchullins.*

CHARLES RICHARD WELD, 1859

Sgurr na h-Uamha and Sgurr nan
Gillean in February, from Ruadh Stac

Page 58/59:
Sgurr Mhic Coinnich and Sgurr
Alasdair from Sgurr Dearg Beag, winter

Left:
Snowstorm on Blaven and Clach Glas
seen from the east at dawn

Clach Glas and Blaven from the north-
west after fresh snow

The mighty Gars-bheinn and Sgurr na
Stri towering above the lodge at
Camasunary

Right:
Two climbers on the south ridge of
Blaven in February, with Sgurr nan
Gillean behind

Left:
Bidean Druim nan Ramh and the
cyclopean headwall of Harta Corrie,
from Sgurr Beag

Sgurr a' Fionn Choire and Am Basteir
from Sgurr Beag

Page 66:
Sgurr a' Ghreadaidh from Sgurr
Dearg Beag

Page 67:
Sgurr na h-Uamha from Sgurr Beag
after fresh snow

Am Basteir and Sgurr a' Fionn Choire
in March, from the west ridge of
Bruach na Frithe

Right:
The west ridge of Bruach na Frithe

Looking south at the Cuillin main
ridge from the summit of Bruach na
Frithe in winter

Reaching the blade-back of Bruach na Frithe
I came in sight of the savageness of the country:
a heavy black-red mantle of the clouds,
the storm winds in their mouths;
about the girdling summits on the awesome scurrs
a dun opening in the firmament
under the low red-black dense pall
of brindled dark surly clouds,
congregation of the horrors of the elements
gathering of the storms for exercise;
hurricane clangour of every blast
about the grim savage pinnacles;
shaking and quivering of the yelling blast
about the battlements of every grey bare-swept summit.

SORLEY MACLEAN

The summit ridge of Sgurr a' Bhasteir
in January

Page 74/75:
The view east from the summit of
Bruach na Frithe, with Sgurr nan
Gillean in the centre, and Blaven far
right

Moonrise over Sgurr a' Fionn Choire,
in March

On the descent from Fionn Choire

Right:
The view out over distant Loch
Harport

Left:
Waterpipe Gully, Sgurr an Fheadain

Frozen Loch Lagan and Sgurr Mhic
Coinnich

On the summit of Sgurr Sgumain after
a sprinkling of late spring snow.
Above: Gars-bheinn, Sgurr nan Eag
and Coir' a' Ghrunnda

Left:
The An Stac screes, Sgurr Dearg and
Sgurr a' Ghreadaidh

The great gabbro wall of Sron na
Ciche catches the evening sun in the
winter

Page 86/87:
Looking out over the sea from upper
Coire Lagan at sunset in the winter

Winter sunset, Coire Lagan

It has been my good fortune to lie on the summit of the Matterhorn and look away across the sea of peaks to Mont Blanc, sixty miles distant; to sit at the old gîte on the Weisshorn, and see the night chase the evening mists up the sides of the Dom and Täschhorn, and to watch the sun rise and flush red over the grand dome of Mont Blanc; but I recall none of these things, beautiful and memorable as they were, so vividly to mind as that perfect night up in lonely Corrie Lagan.

ASHLEY ABRAHAM, 1908

THE ALPINISTS ARRIVE

One of the great secrets that the Cuillin holds is the enormous number and variety of the climbing puzzles that lie encoded, as it were, within the rock, waiting to be unlocked. For the climber, it is the very opposite of a wasteland, or a useless blank on the map. It is an Aladdin's cave of unimaginable riches that is only hinted at in vague, tantalizing glimpses from a distance and can only be entered fully by climbing.

Much of what I've said so far applies to any wild mountain region, though this is admittedly amongst our wildest. What is the special fascination about *this* 'Coolin' beyond all other British mountains?

The answer lies in the particular type of climbing on offer here. For, in climbing terms, as in geological terms, there is nothing else quite like it in Britain. Indeed the very special brand of ridge scrambling found here – as represented by such great lines as the Dubhs Ridge, the Pinnacle Ridge of Sgurr nan Gillean, and the Clach Glas-Blaven traverse – can have few equals in the whole world.

To the first alpinists in the last century, who had no idea that we have, on home ground, mountains as interesting, spectacular, or indeed as difficult as these, the Cuillin was a revelation. Well in advance of his contemporaries was Professor James 'Glacier' Forbes, a distinguished scientist and first Honorary President of the Alpine Club. He was something of a polymath, having the sort of questing spirit that, in Cardinal Newman's words, wants to 'map out the universe.' He did experiments on heat conduction and on the temperature of the Earth at different depths. And he was the first person to really understand the way glaciers move and how, in the process, they sculpt the mountain landscape. He also happened to be the first British mountaineer to make a first ascent of a high Alpine peak, and so he has rightly been called 'the father of British mountaineering.'

On his first trip to Skye in 1836 – in defiance of local folklore, which insisted that it was impossible – he made the first ascent of Sgurr nan Gillean. He was astounded by the quality of the climbing; while admitting that the Cuillin had a greater 'appearance of inaccessibility than perhaps any other mountains in Britain', he said he had 'never seen a rock so adapted for clambering.'

Left:
Sgurr nan Gillean in the winter, from Sgurr Beag

A climber on the Tourist Route of Sgurr nan Gillean, the route which Prof. Forbes used to reach the summit in 1836

91

On the summit ridge of Sgurr nan Gillean

The Pilkington brothers, also of the Alpine Club, who came to Skye for the first time in 1880, must have heard of Forbes's exploit because they made Sgurr nan Gillean their first objective. Having considerable Alpine experience, with many major summits such as the Meije to their credit, they went straight for the north-west face of the main peak – and failed. 'I must say we felt rather small, as an elder brother, who was not an Alpine Climber, was one of the party. We certainly returned with a much greater respect for the mountain than we had when we started in the morning.' It was not long, however, before they had climbed the mountain by all its ridges. But, they said, 'our admiration for it has not faded away . . . It is a climb by whichever way it is ascended, and the summit a real mountain top, a ridge of shattered stone, a jump from which in any direction would relieve you from the payment of your next annual subscription to this Club.' Above all they raved about the beauty of the place. 'We may have seen grander forms in the Alps, and as beautiful colouring in Italy, and we *may* have seen many views of equal loveliness, but know of none to *beat* it for beauty of colour combined with grandeur and variety of form.'

Right:
The Dubhs Ridge, rising 3,000 feet from the shore of Loch Coruisk

Another great Victorian mountaineer, Norman Collie, who climbed extensively in the Alps, the Himalaya and the Rockies, also compared the Cuillin very favourably with the larger ranges:

> The individuality of the Cuillin is not seen in their summits, which are often almost ugly, but in the colour of the rocks, the atmospheric effects, the relative largeness and harmony of the details compared with the actual size of the mountains, and most of all the mountain mystery that wraps them round: not the mystery of clearness such as is seen in the Alps and Himalaya, where range after range recedes into the infinite distance . . . but in the secret beauty born of the mists, the rain, and the sunshine . . .

By 1908 the pioneering rock climber and guidebook writer, Ashley Abraham, was able to report that 'Skye is preferred to Switzerland by many climbers who are intimate with both districts. I count myself amongst these. My memories of the Coolin are more pleasurable and lasting than those of the Alps. The happiness they have brought me has been greater; and in this I am not alone.'

Today, many British climbers would echo these sentiments. For the quintessential Cuillin scramble is right on that fine and uniquely enjoyable borderline between hard scrambling and roped rock climbing, demanding all the concentration and commitment of the latter while retaining the freedom of movement of the former, which is the very essence of climbing – the ability to move freely through vertiginous space, without the encumbrance of ropes. Many climbers would say that, for this reason, this uniquely sensational and exposed scrambling is in some ways even more satisfying than conventional rock climbing with ropes.

Right:
On the final section of the West Ridge of Sgurr Alasdair, above the Mauvais Pas

Apart from the initial trouble in climbing on to the ridge, one may thereafter proceed unroped up broad acres of boiler-plate slabs, whose rock is the roughest gabbro in all the Cuillin. In other words, it is so rough and reliable that only the grossest negligence could bring a man to harm.

W. H. MURRAY, 1947

Climbing the perfect gabbro slabs of the Dubh Ridge

GETTING THE WOBBLIES

The sort of exposed, unroped scrambling that is characteristic of the Cuillin Ridge is one of the most enjoyable and yet at the same time most serious forms of climbing on rock that there is. It is certainly far more serious than the rather childish word 'scramble' would suggest. These are emphatically not 'baby' climbs.

Sadly, there has been a long history of rather questionable understatement here. For example, one of the outstanding 'hard men' of the 1890s, Harold Raeburn, maintained that most of the climbing on Skye was 'ridiculously easy', as the holds were 'firm and plentiful'; and he concluded, disparagingly, that 'the gabbro of the Cuillin is *too* good, it makes one discontented with one's powers on smoother rocks.' (Is it possible he never came across the very smooth basalt?) And recently I met a climber who insisted that the Inaccessible Pinnacle was 'trivial', a curious term, surely, for something which many experienced hill walkers still give a wide berth to, and which people have died on. Frequently, under winter conditions, it fully lives up to its name, even for the very competent. What exactly did he mean? The answer I believe is something on the lines of: 'I am such a good climber that ordinary logic doesn't apply to me.' Why can't people say just how *continually interesting* and *sensational* the climbing on the Main Ridge is – and just how *un*trivial it is at more or less every step! So untrivial, indeed, that thousands of climbers are prepared to drive vast distances to it, year after year.

Starting up the West Ridge of the Inaccessible Pinnacle in damp conditions

While on the subject of understatement I should point out that the word 'walk', as used by some Cuillin guidebooks, bears little resemblance to the normal use of the term. While a scramble is almost by definition something you can fall off, there are still plenty of walks here where you can fall far enough to hurt yourself very badly. The Cuillin is never to be taken lightly. There are just too many places where the slightest error – a slip, or a misjudgement of a loose hold – will almost certainly be fatal. Taking no satisfaction in proving the truth of my argument, I must report that two people lost their lives on the Ridge, in separate accidents, in the time that I was photographing this book.

All the walking and climbing on the Main Ridge is demanding. Perhaps first and foremost it requires good route-finding skills, as the compass is more or less useless here owing to the magnetite in the rock; and in thick cloud, the terrain is potentially so confusing that it is best left well alone by those who are not already familiar with the topography. It also demands a sound sense of judgement of the rock; for the excellent, reassuring gabbro is interspersed with a good deal of much smoother and less reliable dolerite and basalt which can be treacherous in the wet. There is also much loose rock lying on ledges to contend with.

I have on occasions found myself more psychologically extended on some of these loose and exposed slabby ridges, when unroped, than I have been on many much harder, roped climbs. I'm really not exaggerating when I say that I found the modestly graded TD (Thearlaich-Dubh) Gap, climbed in the wet and with big mountain boots, more demanding than a Hard Very Severe I did the next day on dry rock with 'sticky' (rock climbing) boots.

This, then, is adventure climbing with a capital A, and about as far removed as one can possibly get from mere 'sports climbing'. I say 'mere' because that is what 'sports climbers' themselves mean by the term: it is climbing reduced to a single facet, that of being a sport, which of course all climbing is anyway. I have seen a technically advanced sports climber getting the 'wobblies' on a grade 4 scramble here, and I have also recently heard of an experienced alpinist who said he found the Cuillin Ridge more frightening than the Central Pillar of Freney on Mont Blanc.

Far from being trivial, much of the Cuillin Ridge is very intimidating, and perhaps the first quality one needs is an unruffled nature that is not at all easily daunted. A timid approach will almost certainly result in failure. What is required is a very positive attitude and a certain boldness of spirit. Even more than in ordinary rock climbing, one must never be put off by appearances. The quality of the gabbro is such that it is almost invariably easier than it looks from below – often much easier. The

Left:
A climber on the incomparable summit of Clach Glas, the 'Matterhorn of Skye'

route up a daunting rock tower like the summit head wall of Clach Glas, for example, has a wonderful way of 'unfolding'. And again, to an even greater degree than with ordinary rock climbing, the difficulties are reduced considerably by familiarity with the route.

But familiarity will never breed contempt. These are mountains which cannot be tamed. They will never lose their power to instil fear. Many a time when I have been on my own on the Ridge – probing, exploring – I have lost my nerve, and my imagination has started to play tricks with the angle of the rubble-strewn slabs poised over the abyss of Coruisk. Suddenly my fevered mind has seemed to be looking into the jaws of death itself. My legs turn to jelly; I feel both weak and stiff at the same time, and completely out of balance, both physically and mentally.

How well I remember cringing and gibbering like a ninny on the knife-edge ridge leading down to the Basteir Tooth, and my colleague Trefor turning to me and saying, 'Relax, Gordon! Relax!'

This of course is the key to all climbing: to be relaxed – or rather, to be very alert and very relaxed at the same time. The best safety rope – the surest rope – is always oneself, one's inner psyche. The skill of climbing is, above all, a mastery of oneself.

What a fantastic feeling it is when one is moving well, in total control, and actually relishing the difficulties and the danger! This is the incomparable thrill of coping, of being in control in a difficult and potentially dangerous situation. All fears are kept in check by cool precision and bold determination.

Having experienced this, we will understand exactly what the great Victorian alpinist, Mummery, meant when he said that 'the great brown slabs bending over into immeasurable space . . . are old and trusted friends, ever luring us to health and fun and laughter, and enabling us to bid a sturdy defiance to all the ills that time and life oppose.'

As I had no intention of losing either hold or head, there was no risk, and I found that my confidence was not betrayed when I whispered to the rock, "You stick to me, and I'll stick to you." It is, as we all know, the keen enjoyment of such moments that lifts a climb out of the ordinary. It is always a succession of surprises; if the difficulties are seldom great, the problems are none the less interesting, and the chances of sport endless. Besides, there is the ever-present possibility of a fall resulting in a body being, in the words of the Ettrick Shepherd, "dashed on the stanes intil a blash o' bluid." This keeps the wits alive.

FRED W. JACKSON
ON CLACH GLAS IN 1896

Above:
The Pinnacle Ridge of Sgurr nan
Gillean from Coire a' Bhasteir

Left and right:
Abseiling down the south side of the
Third Pinnacle

Only on some of the giant peaks of the Alps are such long stretches of continuously difficult climbing to be had; but it is not every one who cares to incur their attendant drawbacks — the crowded hut, the early morning start, the weary grind over interminable moraine — and these will find an excellent substitute, both as regards quality and length, in the Great Precipice of Sron na Ciche.

ASHLEY ABRAHAM, 1908

Above and left:
Arrow Route, Sron na Ciche

Right:
On Integrity, which continues directly above the slab of Arrow Route

The Cioch, Sron na Ciche

Right:
Looking back at the Cioch from high
in Eastern Gully

The Cioch is wonderfully placed, and its surroundings are strongly reminiscent of the rock-scenery of the Aiguilles of Mont Blanc. Here were the same great sweeps of bare, clean rock, the freedom from vegetation, the airiness of situation, the illimitable fields of air and extraordinary feeling of space. True, there was no glacier at our feet, but breaks in the mist disclosed glimpses of a desolation quite as impressive, while out to the west, stretching away to the infinite distance, the endless waters of the Atlantic seemed to touch the same chord that responds to the beauty of sunlit snow and ice.

ASHLEY ABRAHAM, 1908

3
A WAY OF LIFE

On Sgurr na Stri above Loch Coruisk

Actors often say that the more they go on stage the more frightened they get. Sometimes it seems like that with climbing. There are times when it feels that one has had just too much of this doubt and fear, too much uncertainty, too much exposure to real danger.

Why do we do it? Why do we put ourselves through all this?

The Cuillin is above all a test of *character*, a test of one's worth – as a complete human being. A test, in other words, of how well one can hold oneself together both physically and mentally.

To put it another way, climbing is always a test of faith in oneself: of one's sense of judgement – not just of the rock, but of one's competence to do something that is potentially very dangerous safely and well. Here we face the truth: our competence on this very special and quite dangerous scrambling somehow shows up something much more important. While it may not necessarily be character-building, it is certainly character-revealing! Rather in the same way that the autobiographies of arrogant and self-satisfied politicians expose them for what they are, the Ridge will find us out.

We do not climb because we are sure we can do it. We climb because we *believe* we can do it. We can never be absolutely certain; there are always some doubts. Uncertainty is at the heart of the enterprise: uncertainty about ourselves and uncertainty about the outcome.

Here, in the Cuillin, this is especially the case, where the route-finding tends to be very far from straightforward. The Main Ridge is like a complex, unfolding story-line, full of unexpected twists and turns and not always very pleasant surprises. Often, for example, when approaching a bealach (or col), with all the difficulties apparently successfully accomplished, an unexpected new abyss opens up in front. As Ashley Abraham said, 'such places seem to occur without "rhyme or reason", and with a suddenness that is positively startling.' Classic examples are to be found when descending the Sgurr Thearlaich north ridge to the Bealach Mhic Coinnich, the Bidean Central Peak to the gap between it and the North Peak, An Caisteal to the Bealach Tairneilear, and Clach Glas to the 'Putting Green'.

If the Main Ridge is like a story line, its theme – the central subject – is the unending conflict between our courage and our fear, between our crazy enthusiasm and our rational timidity, our apparent boldness and our inner, fearful imaginings. This is the essence: the way it plays on our fears and our imagination; and, like a strong narrative, a compelling story, it draws us, lures us on.

It is very personal. Only we ourselves can evaluate just how well we measure up to the challenge and satisfy the 'inner daemon', the spark from which all our energy springs. Only the inner self can know exactly what the test has to be. An adventurous project like this can seem to come closer than anything else to the core meaning of one's life. And the landscape is then no longer a meaningless 'Coolin', or wasteland, but a kind of testing ground for the inner self.

An adventure, in its true sense, is something that *comes to* one; it is not an escape *from* anything. By opening ourselves up to all possibilities, we *come to ourselves*. I do not mean that we become egocentric; we simply come closer to finding or rediscovering our real selves. On a great mountain day such as one can have in the Cuillin we emerge from our everyday shell, as the mountains come out of the clouds.

The Ridge is more than simply a great metaphor for life – it is the very embodiment of life, the real thing. These adventures can never be one-off events, condemned to be mythologized by memory; they become a way of life. Here is something we must always keep doing, never stop doing.

Completing the Clach Glas - Blaven traverse: on the final chimney corner on Blaven

Back row – left to right – W.W. KING , W. DOUGLAS , G.P. BAKER.
Sitting – G.A. SOLLY, J. MACLAY, W.W. NAISMITH.
SLIGACHAN – 1898.

GREAT CHARACTERS

The Scottish Mountaineering Club at Sligachan in 1898

When I unashamedly say that the Cuillin is about character, I am thinking particularly of the wonderful assortment of eccentric, individual, and iconoclastic spirits I have encountered on the Ridge. I hold most of them in such high regard that I feel it is almost presumptuous to count myself as one of their number. I think of an extraordinary gallery of characters from a wide range of backgrounds: police drug squad officers, fish farm workers, firemen, film editors, forensic photographers, English lecturers, painters, photography students, botanists, geologists, tree surgeons, Australian tourists, rescue helicopter winch men – all of which is totally irrelevant. The only real thing which matters, which they all have in common, is that adventurous, questing spirit, the spirit that dares, that constantly ventures into new territories.

And I have no reason to think that they are any different in spirit from the first pioneers here – who were a colourful collection of eccentrics, even by Victorian standards. One only has to look at the classic photograph, now in the public bar of the Sligachan Hotel, of the Scottish Mountaineering Club at Sligachan in 1898, to see what I mean. How those personalities shine out of that picture across the decades! They seem at least as interesting as the living people sitting around them in the bar today. There is W.Wickham King, who solved two of the last problems on the Main Ridge: the chimney named after him on Sgurr Mhic Coinnich, and the TD Gap, still the hardest pitch on the entire ridge. Next to him is the glowering and taciturn Godfrey Solly, a solicitor from Merseyside, later Mayor of Birkenhead, who, in 1892, climbed the first Very Severe in the whole country (Eagle's Nest Ridge Direct in the Lake District, even now regarded as 'a bold lead with little protection'.) But the outstanding character here, grinning like a maniac out of the bottom right of the picture, is Willie Naismith, the founder of the Scottish Mountaineering Club. Described by a contemporary as 'a human being of the finest steel, modest and self-effacing', he said it was 'almost a disgrace that any Scotsman whose heart and lungs are in proper order . . . is not more or less of a mountaineer seeing that he belongs to one of the most mountainous countries in the world.' Apart from being an outstanding pioneer of winter mountaineering in Scotland, making an early solo ascent of the Eiger, and giving us his not very useful 'Rule' for timing hill walks (30 minutes per 1000 feet, plus 20 minutes per mile), he made the first direct ascent of the Basteir Tooth in 1898, and for that he will always be immortal.

Arthur arriving on the summit of Clach Glas

These were people who were *driven*, who had the adventurous spark; people with boundless, almost childish enthusiasm, but no self-delusions; who may have had their heads in a cloud of dreams, but who kept their feet firmly on the ground, and their eyes wide open.

Fortunately this spirit is still very much in evidence today in the mountains, particularly in a very traditional area like the Cuillin. It is the spirit of an extraordinary Arthur I met who, on arriving at the top of Clach Glas with an enormous grin on his face, embraced the summit cairn with the words, 'I claim you!' Or of Michael from London, moving calmly, unroped, on the Pinnacle Ridge of Sgurr nan Gillean on his first day ever in the mountains, peering into the abyss – also with a grin on his face – and exclaiming, 'Call that a drop? *Call that a drop?!*' as if the mountain was jesting with him. I'll remember that phrase for ever, and will no doubt use it myself when I'm next in a difficult situation in an exposed position.

THE GLAMAIG HILL RACE, 1993

This annual event, which has been going since 1988, was inspired by the legendary achievement of the Gurkha, Harkabir Thapa, who in 1899 ran up Glamaig from Sligachan and back in 55 minutes. It is is now regarded as one of the finest and toughest of its kind in the country. The four mile round trip, from the Sligachan hotel at sea level to the 775m (2537 ft) summit, involves a one and a half mile approach across a bog followed by very steep grass and scree. In 1993, the weather was the worst ever, with gale force winds and driving rain, but there was no question of it being cancelled. Despite the appalling conditions, the winner completed the race in an amazing 48 minutes 55 seconds, a time he could doubtless have reduced by several minutes in dry conditions. The overall standard was very high, with most of the 57 competitors completing the run in under an hour and a quarter. Although it was a competition, it was actually an extraordinarily high-spirited *group* event; apart from the leading three or four places, it did not seem to matter much in what position people finished. To have taken part in this gruelling test was enough.

Approaching the summit.

Left:
Pat Bonner of the Clydesdale Harriers,
who finished in eighth position,
starting down from the summit

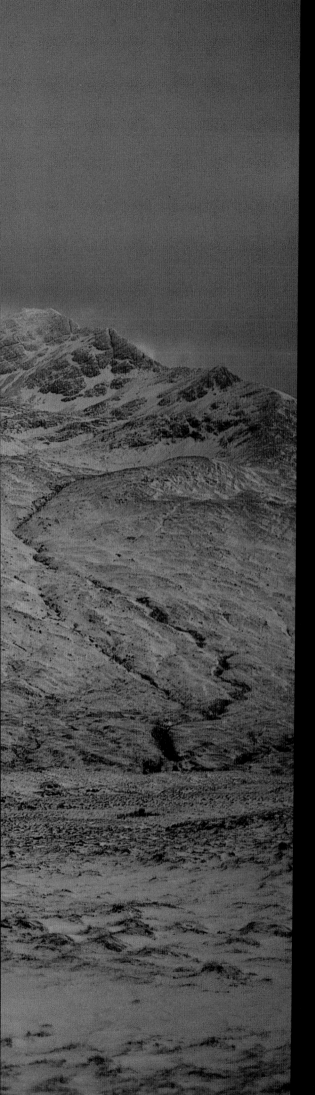

Có seo, có seo oidhche dhona,
Có seo ag coiseachd air a´ mhonadh?
Ceumannan spioraid ri mo thaobh
Agus ceumannan ciùin mo ghaoil,

Ceumannan, ceumannan air na sleibhtean,
Monmhar cheumannan ag éirigh:
Ceumannan fiata, ceumannan ciùine,
Ceumannan iadlaidh socair mùinte.

Có seo, có seo oidhche dunaidh,
Có seo ag coiseachd air a´ mhullach?
Tannasg eanchainne luime nochdte,
Fuar ri aognaidheachd an torchairt.

Who is this, who is this on a bad night,
who is this walking on the moorland?
The steps of a spirit by my side
and the soft steps of my love:

footsteps, footsteps on the mountains,
murmur of footsteps rising,
quiet footsteps, gentle footsteps,
stealthy mild restrained footsteps.

Who is this, who is this on a night of woe,
who is this walking on the summit?
The ghost of a bare naked brain
cold in the chill of vicissitude.

Sgurr nan Gillean, Sgurr a' Bhasteir,
and Bruach na Frithe in February.

Có seo, có seo oidhche 'n spioraid?
Chan eil ach tannasg lom cridhe,
manadh leis fhéin a' falbh a' smaointinn,
cliabh feòil-rùiste air an aonach.

Có seo, có seo oidhche chridhe?
Chan eil ach an nì do-ruighinn,
an samhla a chunnaic an t-anam,
Cuilithionn ag éirigh thar mara.

Có seo, có seo oidhche 'n anama?
a' leanthainn fiaradh an leòis fhalbhaich?
Chan eil, chan eil ach am falbhan
a' sireadh a' Chuilithinn thar fairge.

Có seo, có seo oidhche chinne?
Chan eil ach samhla an spioraid,
anam leis fhéin a' falbh air sléibhtean,
ag iargain a' Chuilithinn 's e 'g éirigh.

Who is this, who is this in the night of the spirit?
It is only the naked ghost of a heart,
a spectre going alone in thought,
a skeleton naked of flesh on the mountain.

Who is this, who is this in the night of the heart?
It is the thing that is not reached,
the ghost seen by the soul,
A Cuillin rising over the sea.

Who is this, who is this in the night of the soul,
following the veering of the fugitive light?
It is only, it is only the journeying one
seeking the Cuillin over the ocean.

Who is this, who is this in the night of mankind?
It is only the ghost of the spirit,
a soul alone going on mountains,
longing for the Cuillin that is rising.

Sgurr nan Gillean from Druim Hain at

Thar lochan fala clann nan daoine,
thar breòteachd blàir is strì an aonaich,
thar bochdainn, caithimh, fiabhrais, àmhghair,
thar anacothrom, eucoir, ainneart, ànraidh,
thar truaighe, eu-dòchas, gamhlas, cuilbheart,
thar ciont is truaillidheachd; gu furachair,
gu treunmhor chithear an Cuilithionn
´s e ´g éirigh air taobh eile duilghe.

Beyond the lochs of the blood of the children of men,
beyond the frailty of the plain and the labour of the mountain,
beyond poverty, consumption, fever, agony,
beyond hardship, wrong, tyranny, distress,
beyond misery, despair, hatred, treachery,
beyond guilt and defilement; watchful,
heroic, the Cuillin is seen
rising on the other side of sorrow.

SORLEY MACLEAN
The Cuillin

'THE CUILLIN OF MANKIND'

I have said that the Cuillin is like a riddle, or an enigma, in that it seems to have some special significance for us which is ultimately beyond our grasp. What is the Cuillin really about? Climbers, of course, are content to say that it has simply been 'put there to be climbed', and that's all there is to it. But *is* that all there is to it? Is it just a giant climbing frame for childish people to play on as an escape from the pressures of modern life? Or has it some arcane, deeper meaning?

I believe that, far from being an escapist indulgence, climbing in the Cuillin is an activity based on values that are of central importance to us. It's an old-fashioned idea. Seen like this, the Cuillin is not a distant irrelevant lump of rock, right on the periphery of life, but a living symbol of all that is good. When asked to explain the importance of climbing, the great Cuillin pioneer, Alexander Nicolson, said, perhaps unsurprisingly, that it allowed 'the full and free exercise of our powers and the cultivation of a bold adventurous spirit' – but then he added, very importantly, 'and any nation which has ceased to think so is on the fair road to decay and degradation.'

Climbing as it is practised here, in a non-competitive spirit, without aids or regulations is, paradoxically, an ultimately civilized pastime, symptomatic of a very advanced level of freedom and enlightenment. It is based on that free-thinking, tolerant spirit which is rooted in a deep respect for the natural world in which we live. It is a supreme affirmation of everything that goes under the much-maligned epithet *liberal*. Far from being an escape, the kind of adventure represented by the Cuillin Ridge is at the forefront of our culture.

In his great poem 'The Cuillin' (1939), Sorley Maclean treats the Ridge as a symbol of fortitude standing 'over a bruised maimed world', in opposition to everything which he describes as 'the frailty of the plain' – that selfish, self-centred demeanour of urban existence which prefers

> . . . ease to energy,
> soft lives to steel-like wills,
> and mole-heaps of morality
> to the eternal hills.

The northern end of the Cuillin Main Ridge, late evening

119

Idealistically and metaphorically, Maclean sees the Cuillin as the final bulwark against the 'surging flood tide' of 'greedy injustice', that is in danger of

> drowning in a great flood of filth
> all that is generous, kind and straight

High above the 'greedy morasses', the Ridge stands, for all time, as a gigantic symbol of the 'watchful, heroic' spirit –

> the lyric Cuillin of the free,
> the ardent Cuillin of the heroic,
> the Cuillin of the great mind.

Seen in this light, the Cuillin is, for Maclean, nothing less than 'The Cuillin of mankind':

> I saw in one living flame
> the surging spirit of man,
> the spirited hero soul,
> the exact brain of the summits,
> the ever triumphant irrepressible spirit,
> the white-darting philosophic heart . . .

Sgurr nan Gillean from the Bhasteir Gorge in March

The summit ridge of Clach Glas, affectionately known as the Imposter

4

THE GREAT TRAVERSE

Long, long and distant,
long the ascent,
long the way of the Cuillin
and the peril of your striving ...

SORLEY MACLEAN

Nearing the summit of Bidean Druim
namh Ramh

THE BRIDGE OF CLIFFS

By the turn of the century climbers were openly considering the feasibility of traversing the whole Cuillin Ridge in one long day. Comprising 18 main summits, 14 of which are over 3000 feet, and never dropping below 2,500 feet in its 7 mile length, it was potentially the longest and finest climb of its type in Britain. Celtic legend has it that the great Ossianic warrior-hero Cuchulain (after whom late nineteenth century Romantics insisted the mountains were named) was the first to take a look. It is said that he managed, as a test of his prowess, to walk across something known as 'the bridge of cliffs' on his first attempt. Whether this was all or part of the Cuillin Ridge is not clear, but the bards were impressed: 'Wonderful was the sight of the bridge afforded, for it narrowed until it became so narrow as the hair of one's head, the second time it shortened till it became as an inch, and the third time it grew slippery as an eel of the river and the fourth time it rose up high as the mast of a ship.' I'm sure any climber who has failed on the Ridge will know just what they meant.

The early pioneers discussed the logistical problems in detail, and many doubted if it was possible. The signs were not particularly encouraging. It had taken the great Norman Collie 18 hours, in 1888, to traverse all the way from Sgurr a'Mhadaidh to Sgurr Thearlaich, where he had been stopped by the TD Gap:

> How many mountains we went over and how many feet we climbed it is impossible to say for in many places we traversed backwards and forwards and up and down in our endeavours to overcome the difficulties that we met with on that extraordinary ridge of the Coolin.

Professor Norman Collie

One of the leading Scottish climbers of the time, William Brown, thought it would be a 'feat of the gods' that would take a minimum of three days, and even Ashley Abraham considered it unlikely that it could be done in one continuous expedition. He doubted 'whether the various qualifications necessary to success will ever be possessed by any one man.' He would have to be something of a superman, with 'exceptional physique and staying power' and an 'intimate knowledge of the entire range . . . Whether the game would be worth the candle, for the attendant risks would be considerable, and whether it is desirable that the Coolin should be treated with such disrespect, are points which each must settle for himself; but personally I think the expressive *Dummheit* of the Swiss guides would justly describe such a performance.'

The first successful traverse by Leslie Shadbolt and A.C. MacLaren on 10 June 1911 was the result of much meticulous planning and careful preparation by two very accomplished climbers. Shadbolt, in particular, was an outstanding rock climber. (Among other things, he made impressive progress on the formidable Deep Gash Gully of Sgurr a'Mhadaidh, which was not eventually climbed until 1949 and is now graded Hard Very Severe). After a brisk 2 hour 15 minute approach from Glenbrittle, Shadbolt and MacLaren completed the traverse of the Main Ridge from Gars-bheinn to Sgurr nan Gillean in a very respectable 12 hours 18 minutes.

It is now completed dozens if not hundreds of times each year, in an average time of about 10 hours between the two end summits – although many people take much longer than this, and a few very advanced fell runners have done it, almost unbelievably, in as little as 3 hours 30 minutes. Experienced rock climbers frequently solo it, using a rope only for abseils – but tackled this way it is, needless to say, for experienced rock climbers only.

At whatever time of year it is tackled, it has an epic quality. As on a great Alpine route, everything about the day is entirely beyond the norm – it is certainly of inordinate length. It should be noted that the distance covered is rather more than the 7 miles usually quoted. The exact length on the map, taking into account all the lateral wiggles and wobbles, is in fact about 6.7 miles, but one needs also to allow for the *upward and downward* dips and rises in the Ridge which probably add another 30% to the actual distance covered; i.e. it is something nearer 9 miles. Add to this 10,000 feet of ascent, and it becomes obvious that the amount of work involved is equal to some of the most formidable routes in the Alps.

If, as on the first traverse, the Ridge is approached from Glenbrittle, without a bivouac, there are about 5 hours of extremely demoralizing, arduous walking *before* the first real technical difficulty (the TD Gap) is reached. After which there are, typically, about eight hours of almost unrelenting interest and seriousness until the summit of Sgurr nan Gillean is reached. And then there is the long tramp of at least two hours back to Sligachan. Leaving Glenbrittle at 6 a.m., for example, an average party cannot realistically expect to arrive at Sligachan much before 9 in the evening, and many will take much longer than this. Indeed, the classic way it is usually done nowadays is to bivvy on Gars-bheinn, which avoids the gruelling start but gives the extra problem of having to carry bivvy gear on the traverse, when the object is to keep weight to a minimum. Then there is the additional problem of water, which will of course be a major

High on the east ridge of Gars-bheinn,
above Loch Scavaig

consideration on a hot summer day. The only reliable source on
the Ridge itself is about two hundred feet down on the north side
of Sgurr a'Fionn Choire, just before the Basteir Tooth is reached;
unless water has already been stashed at strategic places on the
Ridge, at least three litres per person will have to be carried.
(Technical details of the route may be found in the Appendix.)

Most of the logistical details are so well-known to the average
Cuillin enthusiast that it may seem that I'm labouring the point.
But the fact is that an extraordinarily high proportion of
contenders fail on it, and a disappointingly high number of those
who succeed say 'Never again!' Which only goes to show that the
Ridge is frequently underestimated, and that most of these people
would clearly have been better advised to have done parts of it
first. Actually, a great many do just that, and spend many days,
and even years, exploring and learning the Ridge. There is then
the rather different fascination of linking it all together – like
reacquainting oneself with a motley collection of old friends, and
maybe a few enemies, in quick succession.

To my mind, the style in which the Ridge is traversed is all-
important. The ideal, surely, is to do it so well that one would be
only too glad to repeat it – perhaps many times. The purist will
want to follow the crest exclusively, taking in all the natural
challenges it throws up, but the overriding object must be to do it,
if not as fast as possible, certainly as fluently as possible.

Climbing the Cuillin Ridge well has something in common
with playing a long and difficult piece of music: it's like trying to
follow a beautiful melodic line through space – sometimes simple,
sometimes very intricate – accomplishing all the technical
difficulties and obstacles as smoothly as possible. It's about flow
and pace and rhythm. To any climber going well there will always

be a sense of urgency, an awareness of the relentless march of time, and the need to play the difficult chords without dithering, without ever breaking the tempo. Onwards, ever onwards, to the climax of Am Basteir and its Tooth, the final peroration of the West Ridge, and the long, languid coda across the bogs to Sligachan.

But there will also be the quieter passages, the crucial rests, the stops for water, relishing the silence. 'Unhurried speed' is the key; to be relaxed while moving fast; everything done with an easy precision: not a foot out of place, not a single loose hold dislodged.

The nearer one can approach this ideal, the more smoothly one can move, far from feeling frightened or 'pushed' one will have a deep sense of inner contentment. One may even begin to understand what Gaston Rébuffat meant when he said that a climber who is moving well 'is aware of a quiet satisfaction, as if he were receiving a silent approval. In such a way does spring-water, born of the earth, flow gently, embracing the banks.'

The main ridge at dusk, from the summit of Gars-bheinn

... Long, but come it will,
the golden run will come to us;
the Cuillin will rise,
genial in his white glory;
though the night is bitter to us
that cast a black shadow on the beauty,
the morning will break
on splendid battlements.

SORLEY MACLEAN

Above and right:
Sunrise on the summit of Gars-bheinn

Mike Lates leaving the summit of
Gars-bheinn at 7.00 am to do the
Greater Traverse – the whole Cuillin
Ridge, plus Garbh-bheinn, Clach Glas
and Blaven.

Left: Abseiling into the Thearlaich-Dubh Gap.

Above: Climbing out of the TD Gap on the north side: the hardest pitch on the Cuillin Ridge

Below: Completing the TD Gap, with the southern end of the main ridge behind.

Looking back at the summits of Sgurr Thearlaich and Sgurr Alasdair on the traverse of the main ridge. Since Sgurr Alasdair lies just west of the main ridge, a short detour has to be made from Sgurr Thealaich in order to take in the highest summit in the Cuillin.

The highest point is now called after Sheriff Nicolson, the peak on the main ridge to the north-east of Sgurr Alasdair being named Sgurr Tearlach, in honour of Mr. Charles Pilkington. These black monoliths commemorate the names of two men whose exploits will ever be interwoven with the history of the Coolin. And what a fitting reward is theirs! What proud monuments they possess! How different these pedestals of gabbro with their crowns of basaltic lava keeping watch over the lonely corries, and washed by the salt rains and cleansing winds of the broad Atlantic, from those statues built by men's hands and besmirched with the grime and soot of our great cities!

ASHLEY ABRAHAM, 1908

Page 134/135:
The superbly exposed Collie's Ledge
on Sgurr Mhic Coinnich. Behind on
the left can be seen An Stac which, if
climbed directly up the crest, provides
one of the best sections of serious
scrambling on the entire ridge.
Directly beyond it lies the Inaccessible
Pinnacle (above).

The East Ridge of the Inaccessible
Pinnacle

Left:
Looking back along Collie's Ledge
towards Sgurr Alasdair

The East Ridge of the Inaccessible
Pinnacle, Sgurr Dearg, with An Stac
below on the right and Blaven behind

*The pinnacle, rising precipitously
for over a hundred feet on the
South side, falls in one
perpendicular drop of 300 or 400
feet on the North. As the mountain
on which it stands also shoots
steeply away on either side, the eye
seems to plunge immediately to the
bottom of Glen Coruisk, 2,500 feet
below, giving an additional feeling
of insecurity to anyone who,
clinging to the narrow East edge,
feels the whole slab vibrate with the
blow of a falling rock that he has
levered out from the crest above, as
actually happened to me on the
first ascent. Very great care and
labour were required to pull out
stones, loose but still forming part
of the natural rock, and often the
whole of the edge, which by the
way is only six inches to a foot
wide in many places.*

CHARLES PILKINGTON, 1888

Abseiling down the west ridge of the
Inaccessible Pinnacle

Onlookers on the summit of Sgurr
Dearg

Having a short rest on the summit of
An Caisteal

*On fine days one can take one's ease on the Coolin, and should one weary
of rock-scrambling one can sit on some ledge perched high up above the
lower world, surrounded by huge crags making foregrounds full of
strength and beauty, and looking out over low-lying moors to the outer
islands, that seem to belong to some mysterious land in the far-off west.*

PROF NORMAN COLLIE, 1907

Left:
Looking south and north from the
summit of Sgurr Mhadaidh. Loch
Coruisk three thousand feet below.

Right:
Abseiling off the Basteir Tooth in bad
conditions

The Basteir Tooth, the last difficult
obstacle on the Great Traverse

Am Basteir and the Basteir Tooth in a
heat wave

On the West Ridge of the Inaccessible Pinnacle

THE MAGIC OF LONG DAYS

I have not lost the magic of long days;
I live them, dream them still . . .

Geoffrey Winthrop Young

For all the suffering, fear, and disappointments with the weather, the best mountain days in the Cuillin have a truly magic quality. The *intensity* of the experience is such that it operates at many levels: the physical and the psychological, the real and the imagined, the rational and the intuitive, the crafty and the crazy, the timeless and the urgent, the poetic and the muscular. And, again like a great piece of music, what an extraordinary mixture of emotions it involves! What a blend of fear and excitement – what a mixture of beauty and danger, and of meticulous precision and physical freedom!

Perhaps, in the end, the precise route or routes one does are not so important as the quality of the whole day. The greatest days have a revelatory ambience in which the whole landscape, and all the characters in it, suddenly seem to belong to a world outside ordinary time. As the day unfolds and the adrenalin of obstacles faced and overcome gives way to the euphoria of success, everyone starts to bubble with an overflowing enthusiasm for the sheer quality of the experience. Something extraordinary is for a while drawn out of us by the landscape, just as the landscape itself is transformed by the quality of the atmosphere and the light. For a magic hour the sun beams down on us and we move in a timeless state that is worth countless hours of normal life. Stronger for it, we continue to wend our problematic and precarious way through life, space walking on the edge of our dreams, with laughter in our hearts and as free as the winds of heaven.

On the summit of Bruach na Frithe in winter

Page 146/147:
Mike Lates on the summit of Blaven, having completed the Greater Traverse, 11 1/4 hours after leaving Gars-bheinn (see page 128).

Page 150/151:
Sgurr Sgumain, Sgurr Alasdair, and Sgurr Thearlaich from the summit of Sgurr Dubh na Da Bheinn, late evening

Gas hisses towards a dusk coffee.
We haven't said much all day,
mostly selected individual lines,
soaked up views, negotiated rock.
We talk briefly and sip hot liquid
in a quiet euphoria at being here.
In the west is an improbable light,
thin horizontal fireworks on the Minch
slowly evolving like a sixties lightshow.
Our finger ends sing
from the abrasion of gabbro.

I lie awake, not cold, not troubled by midges,
mulling over all the nuances
of our mountain days. Finally,
turning again to fit the gabbro,
the last thing I am aware of is
two trajectories, drifting,
parabolas into the future,
a little unsure of their destinations.

KEVIN BORMAN, 1993

Watching the sunset from the summit
of Sgurr nan Eag

Sgurr nan Gillean at dusk, from Sgurr
a' Bhasteir

The dream remains ...
Looking back towards cloud-capped
Skye from Loch Hourn on the
mainland at sunset

GLEN BRITTLE

Loch Brittle   Car Park   Glenbrittle

Sgurr nan Gobhar

Coire a' Ghreadaidh

Sgurr na Banachdich

Inaccessible
Pinnacle   Coire na
Sgurr Dearg   Banachdich   Sgurr a' Ghreadaidh

Coire na   Sgurr
Banachdich   Thormaid

An Stac

Coire Lagan

Sgurr Alasdair   Sgurr Mhic Choinnich   Bidei

Sgurr Sgumain   Coire an Uaigneis
                      Sgurr Thearlaich

T D Gap   Coireachan Ruadha

Sgurr Dubh na Da Bheinn

Sgurr Dubh Mor   Sgurr Coire an Lochain

Caisteal a' Garbh-choire

Sgurr nan Eag   Coire an Lochain

Sgurr a' Choire Bhig

Sgurr Dubh Beag

Gars-bheinn   Druim nan Ramh

An Garbh-choire

Mad Burn   Loch Coruisk

Coire Riabhach

Coruisk Memorial Hut

Scavaig River   Sgurr Hain

Steeping Stones

Sgurr na Stri

Loch Scavaig

The Bad Step

Blaven (B

Loch na Creitheach

Camasunary

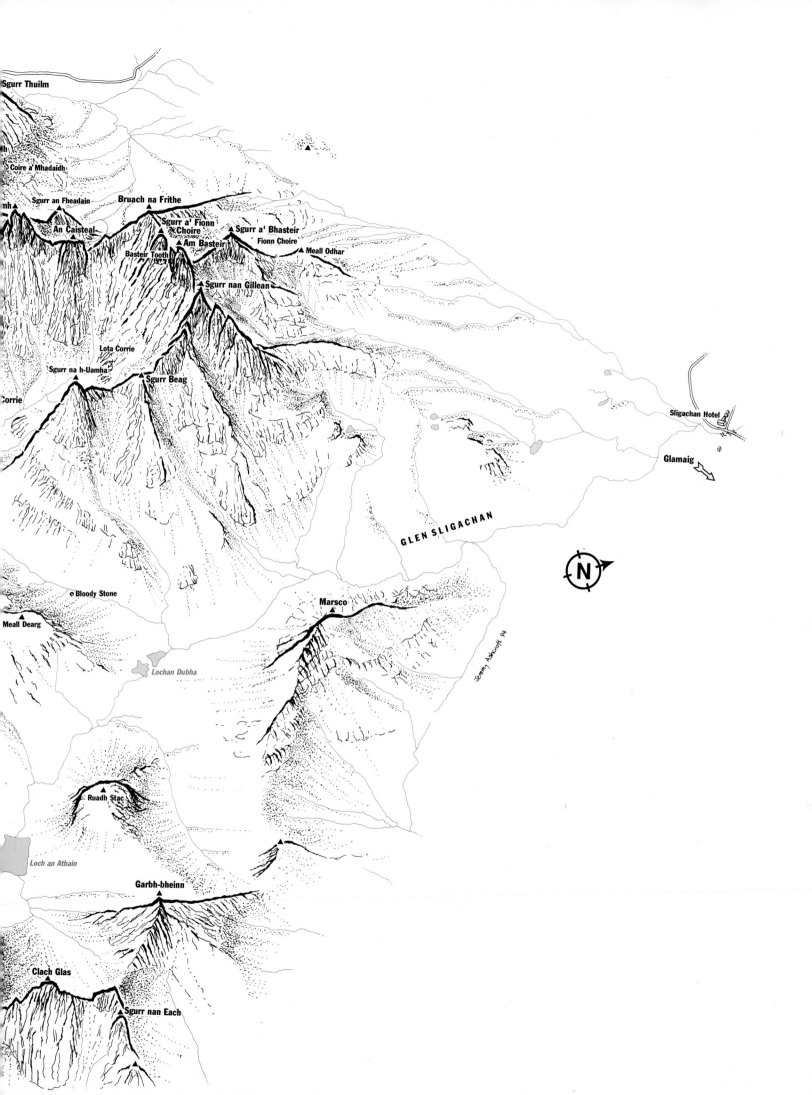

Sgurr Thuilm

Coire a' Mhadaidh

Sgurr an Fheadain Bruach na Frithe

An Caisteal Sgurr a' Fionn
Choire Sgurr a' Bhasteir

Basteir Tooth Am Basteir Fionn Choire

Meall Odhar

Sgurr nan Gillean

Lota Corrie

Sgurr na h-Uamha Sgurr Beag

Corrie

Sligachan Hotel

Glamaig

GLEN SLIGACHAN

N

Bloody Stone

Marsco

Meall Dearg

Lochan Dubha

Jeremy Ashcroft 94

Ruadh Stac

Loch an Athain

Garbh-bheinn

Clach Glas

Sgurr nan Each

THE CUILLIN SUMMITS

Sgurr Alasdair	3,257 ft (993m)	*Skorr Alastair*	Alexander's Peak	2S
The Inaccessible Pinnacle	3,234 ft (986m)			RI
Sgurr Dearg	3,209 ft (978m)	*Skoor Jerrak*	Red Peak	1S
Sgurr Thearlaich	3,208 ft (977m)	*Skoor Cheerlach or Hairlach*	Charlie's Peak	3S
Sgurr a' Ghreadaidh	3,192 ft (973m)	*Skoor a Hreeta (or Gretty)*	Peak of the Thrashings	3S
Sgurr nan Gillean	3.167 ft (965m)	*Skoor nun Gillyan*	Peak of the Gullies, or Boys	3S
Sgurr na Banachdich	3,166 ft (965m)	*Skoor na Banyerdich*	Smallpox Peak	W
Bruach na Frithe	3,143 ft (958m)	*Brooach na Free*	Slope of the Forest	1S
An Stac	3,125 ft (952m)	*Un Stahk*	The Stack	2S
Sgurr Mhic Coinnich	3,111 ft (948m)	*Skoor Vick-cunyuch*	Mackenzie's Peak	2S
Sgurr Sgumain	3,108 ft (947m)	*Skoor Skooman*	Mound or Stack Peak	1S
Sgurr Dubh Mor	3,096 ft (944m)	*Skoor Doo Mor*	Big Black Peak	2S
Sgurr Dubh na Da Bheinn	3,078 ft (938m)	*Skoor Doo na Darven*	Black Peak of the Two Mountains	2S
Am Basteir	3,070 ft (936m)	*Um Basiter (or Bastyer)*	The Executioner	3S
Sgurr a' Fionn Choire	3,068 ft (935m)	*Skoor a Feeon Corrie*	Peak of the Fair Corrie	2S
Blaven	3,044 ft (928m)	*Blarven*	Blue Mountain	1S
Sgurr Thormaid	3,040 ft (927m)	*Skoor Toramid or Horrormidge*	Norman's Peak	3S
Sgurr nan Eag	3,031 ft (924m)	*Skoor nan Ache*	Notched Peak	1S
Sgurr a' Mhadaidh	3,012 ft (918m)	*Skoor a Vatty*	Peak of the Foxes	2S
Basteir Tooth	3,005 ft (916m)	*Basteer Tooth*	Executioner Tooth	RI
Sgurr a' Bhasteir	2,951 ft (899m)	*Skoor a Vashtur or Vasiter*	Peak of the Executioner	W
Gars-bheinn	2,935 ft (895m)	*Garsven*	Echoing Mountain	W
Sgurr Thuilm	2,885 ft (879m)	*Skoor Hoolim*	Peak of Tulm, or ?William	1S
Sgurr a' Choire Bhig	2,872 ft (875m)	*Skoor a'Horrie Vick*	Peak of the Little Corrie	1S
Bidean Druim nan Ramh	2,850 ft (869m)	*Beedjen Drim nan Rarve*	Pinnacle of the Ridge of Oars	RI
Sgurr na Bhairnich	2,826 ft (861m)	*Skoor na Vannich*	Peak of the Limpet	1S
Sron na Ciche	2,817 ft (859m)	*Strawn na Keecha*	Promontory of the Nipple	W
An Caisteal	2,730 ft (832m)	*Un Casteal*	The Castle	2S
Caisteal a' Garbh-choire	2,719 ft (829m)	*Casteal a Garrav-horrie*	Castle of the Rough Corrie	RI
Sgurr Eadar da Choire	2,650 ft (808m)	*Skoor Aya-dada horrie*	Peak between Two Corries	1S
Garbh-bheinn	2,644 ft (806m)	*Garven*	Rough Mountain	1S
Clach Glas	2,582 ft (787m)	*Clach Glass*	Grey Stone	RI
Glamaig	2,525 ft (770m)	*Glamaig*	Gorge Mountain	W
Sgurr Beag	2,511 ft (765m)	*Skoor Bake*	Little Peak	1S
Sgurr Coir' an Lochain	2,491 ft (759m)	*Skoor Corran Lochan*	Peak of the Corrie Loch	2S
Sgurr na h-Uamha	2,416 ft (736m)	*Skoor na Hooa*	Peak of the Cave	3S
Marsco	2,414 ft (735m)	*Marsco*	Seagull Rock	W
Sgurr Dubh Beag	2,403 ft (732m)	*Skoor Doo Bake*	Little Black Peak	RI
Beinn Dearg Mhor	2,403 ft (732m)	*Ben Jerrak Voar*	Big Red Mountain	W
Beinn an Caillich	2,401 ft (731m)	*Ben na Calyach*	Mountain of the Old Woman	W
Sgurr nan Each	2,350 ft (716m)	*Skoor nan Yech*	Peak of the Horses	2S
Beinn Dearg Mhor, Broadford	2,325 ft (709m)	*Ben Jerrak Voar*	Big Red Mountain	W
Sgurr an Fheadain	2,253 ft (686m)	*Skoor an Fetchun (or Aityan)*	Peak of the Waterpipe	2S
Belig	2,250 ft (686m)	*Baylig*	Birch Tree Bark	W
Beinn Dearg Mheadhonach	2,139 ft (652m)	*Ben Jerrak Vee'onach*	Middle Red Mountain	W
Sgurr nan Gobhar	2,069 ft (631m)	*Skoor nan Gohar or Goer*	Peak of the Goat	1S
Beinn Dearg Bheag	1,916 ft (584m)	*Ben Jerrak Vake*	Little Red Peak	W
Beinn na Cro	1,883 ft (574m)	*Ben na Craw*	Mountain of the Raven	W
Glas Bheinn Mhor	1,871 ft (570m)	*Glassven Voar*	Big Grey Mountain	W
Ruadh Stac	1,750 ft (533m)	*Rooag Stahk*	Red Stack	W
Sgurr na Stri	1,631 ft (497m)	*Skoor na Stree*	Peak of Strife	W

GRADING SYSTEM

The grading system (in the right-hand column) is a modified version of that used by J.Wilson Parker in his excellent and generally reliable guide 'Scrambles in Skye' published by the Cicerone Press. Briefly, the grades, as used here, may be summed up as follows. The defining characteristic of a 'walk' (**W**) is that the hands may be kept safely in the pockets, but only in that respect does it bear any resemblance to what is normally meant by the term, for the ground may be very steep and the work involved extremely toilsome (anyone disputing this is cordially invited to reacquaint themselves with Gars-bheinn). The scrambling grades have been re-aligned to tally with those used in most other scrambling guides (e.g 'Scrambles in Lochaber' by Noel Williams, 'Scrambles in the Lake District' by R.B. Evans, and 'Scrambles in Snowdonia' by Steve Ashton.) However, in the Cuillin it is rather more difficult to make a clear distinction between the grades as many of even the easiest scrambles are in places very exposed. All that can be said with any confidence is that they represent a progressively higher level of technical difficulty and seriousness, such that inexperienced scramblers may find a rope necessary on a Grade 3 scramble. A rock climb (denoted by an **R** in my classification) is a route which demands a certain level of *technical* skill, in addition to strength and balance, in order to stay in contact with the rock: scramblers with no experience of rock-climbing are definitely advised to use a rope on the most difficult sections of these. And all but the most experienced and competent rock climbers will certainly use a rope on rock routes of grade III and above, on first acquaintance. The Roman numeral aligns with the UIAA classification, as shown below:

	Parker grades	UIAA grades	British rockclimbing grades
W	2W		
1S			
	3S		
2S			
3S	4S		
RI	RI	I	Easy – Moderate
	RII		Moderate
RII		II	Moderate – Difficult
	RIII		Difficult
RIII	RIV	III	Hard Difficult – Very Difficult
RIV		IV	Hard Very Difficult – Severe

For details on the rock-climbing and scrambling guidebooks, see the Bibliography.

A GRADED LIST OF THE BEST ROUTES TO THE MAIN CUILLIN SUMMITS

This is in effect an updated version of Ashley Abraham's 'graduated list of courses' in his classic 'Rock-climbing in Skye' of 1908. It consists exclusively of routes to summits in the Black Cuillin (though Marsco is admittedly a very borderline case, having only a short section of gabbro on its south ridge). It also excludes rock climbs that are climbed for their own sake and not primarily as a means of reaching a summit. Unlike the graded lists in rock-climbing guidebooks, this list should be construed much less as an indication of technical difficulty than of the overall scale of the undertaking, taking into account such additional factors as seriousness, exposure, route-finding difficulties, quality of the rock and the length of the route. As with all such lists, it is not to be taken very seriously; like Ashley Abraham, 'I do not for a moment expect everybody to agree with my classification; indeed, I doubt not that much obloquy will fall to its portion.' I am also well aware that a number of placings are controversial to say the least – but what is the point of such lists if they do not provoke debate and hopefully a fresh appraisal of certain routes?

The star rating system that is used is similar to that which is commonly used in rock-climbing guidebooks – the three levels of excellence being roughly equivalent to: good, very good, and a total classic of its type. A **D** after a route means that it is recommended as a descent route, with the added implication that it provides a gruelling means of ascent (but one man's poison is, I suppose, another man's meat.)

W	Sgurr na Banachdich via Coir' an Eich	
	Sgurr Sgumain via the west shoulder of Sron na Ciche	
	Sgurr a' Bhasteir from Bealach nan Lice	
	Gars-bheinn via the south-east ridge	*
	Gars-bheinn via the south-west spur	
1S	Bruach na Frithe via Fionn Choire	*
	Marsco, south ridge, from Coire nam Bruadaran	*
	Blaven, Normal Route from Loch Slapin	*
	Sgurr Thuilm	
	Blaven, south-east spur	**D**
	Blaven, south ridge	**
	Sgurr Dearg via Bealach Coire na Banachdich and the north ridge	
	Sgurr Sgumain via Sgumain Stone Shoot	
	Garbh-bheinn and Belig from Coire nam Bruadaran	**
	Bruach na Frithe, north-west ridge	*
	Sgurr Dearg, west ridge	*
2S	Sgurr Dearg via the An Stac screes	
	Sgurr a' Bhasteir, north-east ridge	**
	Sgurr a' Bhasteir, north-west ridge	*
	The traverse of Sgurr Dubh na Da Bheinn	*
	Sgurr a' Fionn Choire, travers	
	Garbh-bheinn south-east ridge, via Sgurr nan Each	**

	Sgurr na Banachdich via Sgurr nan Gobhar	**D****
	Sgurr na Banachdich via Bealach Coire na Banachdich	
	Sgurr nan Eag via Coir' a' Ghrunnda and the north ridge (taken direct)	*
	Gars-bheinn to Sgurr Dubh na Da Bheinn	**
	An Caisteal via Bealach Harta	
	Sgurr Alasdair via the Great Stone shoot	**D**
	Bruach na Frithe via Tairneilear Stone Shoot and Sgurr na Bhairnich	**D**
	Sgurr Dubh Mor via Sgurr Dubh na Da Bheinn	*
	Sgurr a'Mhadaidh via An Dorus	
	Sgurr Mhic Coinnich via An Stac screes and the north-west ridge	***D**
	Sgurr Mhic Coinnich via Bealach Mhic Coinnich and Collie's Ledge	**
3S	Sgurr nan Gillean, south-east ridge from Sligachan (the Tourist Route)	**
	Sgurr Alasdair via Sgurr Sgumain and the 'Easy Way' (round the Mauvais Pas)	*
	Sgurr a' Ghreadaidh via An Dorus	
	Sgurr a' Mhadaidh via Sgurr Thuilm	**
	Sgurr Thearlaich via head of the Great Stone shoot	
	Traverse of Sgurr Ghreadaidh to Sgurr na Banachdich	**
	Sgurr Thearlaich via Bealach Mhic Coinnich	
	Am Basteir, east ridge	
	North Peak of Bidean Druim nan Ramh via Bealach Harta, direct	*
	Sgurr na h-Uamha via Sgurr Beag	*
RI	West Ridge of Sgurr nan Gillean via the Gendarme Shoulder	**
	West Ridge of Sgurr nan Gillean via Nicolson's chimney	
	Traverse of An Caisteal from the head of the Tairneilear Stone Shoot	*
	Central Peak of Bidean via Sgurr Fheadain and the South-West Peak	**
	An Stac, East Ridge Direct	***
	Basteir Tooth, Collie's Route	**
	Inaccessible Pinnacle, East Ridge	***
	Pinnacle Ridge, Sgurr nan Gillean	***
RII	Traverse of the four tops of Sgurr a' Mhadaidh from south to north	**
	Sgurr Mhic Coinnich via King's Chimney	**
	Clach Glas – Blaven Traverse	***
	The Dubhs Ridge	***
	Sron na Ciche via the Cioch and Eastern Gully	**
RIII	The Traverse of Bidean Druim nan Ramh	**
	Inaccessible Pinnacle, West Ridge	*
RIV	Sgurr Alasdair South-West Ridge direct via the Mauvais Pas	**
	Am Basteir via Naismith's Route and 'The Mouth' direct	***
	Sgurr Thearlaich via the Thearlaich-Dubh Gap	**

THE TRAVERSE OF THE CUILLIN MAIN RIDGE

Approach

Gars-bheinn

From Glenbrittle, follow the main Coire Lagan path over the first rise. Just before the stream on the R enters a miniature gorge, branch off R on another obvious path. Follow this often very boggy and increasingly indistinct path all the way past Coir' a' Ghrunnda and Coire nan Laogh before striking up the steep flanks of Gars-bheinn, taking advantage of whatever grassy patches may be found amongst the laborious scree. To continue the traverse all the way round to the end of the Main Ridge proper, overlooking Loch Scavaig, is only marginally less arduous, and much further, but it is unquestionably finer aesthetically. Since both these routes can only be described as demoralizing, many people prefer to reach Gars-bheinn via the southern section of the Main Ridge from Sgurr nan Eag (which is best approached very directly by going over the Sgumain Stone Shoot on the north side of Sron na Ciche and then descending to Loch Coir' a' Ghrunnda, rather than by the very long and usually boggy path round into Coire Ghrunnda from Glenbrittle.) This is a much more attractive proposition, and has the added advantage that water may be stashed at a strategic point on the ridge; it does mean, however, that the southern part of the ridge has to be traversed twice, a concept which the purist may find objectionable.

Perhaps the finest, classic way of doing the Traverse is from Coruisk, reached by boat from Elgol. Here there is the advantage of the distance to Gars-bheinn being reduced by one third. The summit may be reached via a scree gully at the head of Coire Beag, or from the shoulder 200m south-east of the summit, gained from Coir' a' Chruidh. The approach to either of these routes via the Mad Burn is not as straightforward as one may imagine and, if one is bivvying at Coruisk rather than on Gars-bheinn, is well worth reconnoitering the night before to avoid making time-wasting mistakes in the early hours.

A limited number of not very comfortable bivvy sites may be found at the summit of Gars-bheinn; better sites exist a little way down the Main Ridge towards Sgurr a' Choire Bhig.

The Great Traverse

Sgurr a' Choire Bhig
Sgurr nan Eag
Caisteal a' Garbh-choire

A mile and a half of fine ridge-walking and easy scrambling (W–2S), in a superb position above the sea, leads from the summit of **Gars-bheinn** over **Sgurr a' Choire Bhig** and **Sgurr nan Eag** to Bealach a' Garbh-choire. The imposing turret of **Caisteal a' Garbh-choire** may be climbed directly up the S side by Moderate (RII) rock-climbing on superb rough peridotite; at the far (north) end turn sharp L and descend on the west side. Many people will circumvent the Caisteal completely (most easily by a path a little way down on the R, Garbh-choire, side). Continue by easy but butch 2S scrambling on blocky peridotite over **Sgurr Dubh na Da Bheinn** to Bealach Coir' an Lochain. (At the summit, the ridge turns L; in the mist this bouldery wilderness could give route-finding problems.)

Sgurr Dubh na Da Bheinn

The whole route so far is really just a long introduction, much tamer in character than the rest of the Main Ridge. This southern section is, however, one of the finest ridge traverses of its standard in the British Isles; its fate is to be a preamble to something much greater. At the Bealach Coir' an Lochain the difficulties begin in earnest: as Croz said to Whymper on the first ascent of the Matterhorn, 'Now for something altogether different'!

The TD Gap

Shortly after leaving the Bealach a steep and exposed wall on the L side of the ridge is climbed on good holds (RI) to the summit of the pinnacle forming the south side of the **TD (Thearlaich-Dubh) Gap**. Abseil 30 ft (9m) into the gap, then climb the opposite (north-west) wall by a very steep and polished chimney-groove, 80 ft (24m), RIV. It has sufficient holds, except where it most matters, and is the hardest pitch on the entire ridge.

Sgurr Alasdair

In order to climb **Sgurr Alasdair**, the highest peak in the Cuillin, which lies just off the Main Ridge, a short detour has to be made. At a levelling about 100 ft (30m) above the TD Gap, follow an easy traverse line L-wards into the Great Stone Shoot. On the opposite side of the scree, scramble up the obvious south-east ridge (2S) to the very fine, exposed summit; then retrace one's steps to the top of the Stone Shoot.

Many people avoid the TD Gap completely by leaving the Ridge at the Bealach Coir' an Lochain and traversing L across the scree below the crags of Sgurr Thearlaich to climb Sgurr Alasdair by the south-west flank (the **'Easy Way'**, 3S, R of the 'Mauvais Pas'). This is actually not such a cheat as it sounds, and there is the advantage of making a neat traverse of Sgurr Alasdair, without having to retrace one's steps. It is certainly a good alternative in damp conditions.

Sgurr Thearlaich

From the top of the Great Stone Shoot, the west wall of the summit of **Sgurr Thearlaich** is awkward to start, and is best tackled by a short vertical groove (RI) about 20 ft (6m) down on the south side, after which steep scrambling (3S) leads directly to the Main Ridge just south of the summit.

From the summit of Sgurr Thearlaich, walk down the fine roof-crest ridge towards Bealach Mhic Coinnich. A short section of scrambling leads to a cleft and then to a broad promontory with sheer drops on all sides. The ridge may be descended directly by abseil, or by insecure, polished slabs slightly on the Coruisk side (at least RI). A clever and rather unobvious route avoids these difficulties on the R (Coruisk) side by taking a faint grassy traverse path from the above-mentioned cleft. This leads to an open corner, and then to a short, exposed wall, which is quite easy (3S), but only if the best line is found. Easy ground is then followed round to the R to the Bealach Mhic Coinnich. Most commonly used nowadays, however, is a much looser and more time-consuming route on the Coire Lagan side of 3S standard, which owing to the amount of traffic it has seen is probably the safest bet. With careful route-finding all the loose rock can be avoided. The start is not at all obvious: on the L side of the north end of the promontory is a very steep V-groove. Move down the short spur to the L of this about 20 ft (6m) to a narrow notch. Pass through this and climb down an exposed rib on good holds to a traverse line which leads round to a broad sloping slab backed by a sheer wall. Cross this with care (best line quite high) to reach the top of a wide scree-filled gully. Climb down friable rock on the R (north) side of this, and then a steep subsidiary groove on the R side of a prominent rib until easy ground is reached below the level of the Bealach Mhic Coinnich. Traverse easily round and up to the Bealach.

Sgurr Mhic Coinnich

From the Bealach, move R (east) 20 ft (6m) to a short steep wall which gives access, on big holds, to the start of Collie's Ledge slanting up to the L. The most direct and proper way to the summit of **Sgurr Mhic Coinnich** is up the obvious, rather intimidating corner of **King's Chimney** in the south face, reached by a short scramble from Collie's Ledge. It is, however, much easier than it looks, with good holds, on perfect gabbro.

Climb the corner to the overhang, which is avoided on the R wall (RI). A softer, unroped option is to follow the exceptionally fine **Collie's Ledge** (2S) round onto the north-west ridge of the mountain, and then to double back to the summit by a short section of exposed and thought-provoking scrambling. The lower part of the north-west ridge to the Bealach Coire Lagan provides straightforward, secure scrambling on sound rock (2S).

An Stac

Beyond the Bealach Coire Lagan rises the imposing bastion of **An Stac**. This can be bypassed completely on the L by a slabby, scree-covered rake (2S) which has little to recommend it and misses one of the best bits of scrambling on the entire ridge. An introductory section to the direct route is started by a difficult diagonal line just L of the notch at the north-west end of the Bealach (RI). The L side of the ridge is now followed on loose rock to a small col below the 450 ft (140m) tower of An Stac proper. (A scree shoot to the L provides an escape route back to the rake for those who have second thoughts about what lies ahead, for there are no ways off above.) Despite its traditional reputation of being 'disgustingly loose', all loose rock can be avoided. As with so much of the Cuillin Ridge the secret is to keep very close to the extremely exposed crest (the best line lies just to its L), which has been picked bare like a skeleton, and consists of very compact dolerite with plenty of good solid holds but very few incuts (RI, sustained). Shortly before the summit, a narrowing rib leads to a horizontal grassy ledge. Either traverse horizontally L 12 ft (4m) to reach a loose, easy rake slanting up to the L, which is best quit in favour of the easy-angled crest on the R leading to the summit; or, follow the amazingly exposed ledge round to the R above the abyss of Coir'-uisg to emerge, after one tricky step at its end, just beyond the summit of An Stac.

The Inaccessible Pinnacle

Straight ahead, beyond an easy 2S scramble along a narrow horizontal crest, lies the superlative **East Ridge of the Inaccessible Pinnacle**, 150ft (45m), (RI). Those who have soloed An Stac will probably be confident enough to continue unroped for, while it is even more exposed, its narrow crest is covered with a profusion of incut (but very polished) holds. On the far side of the precariously poised summit block known as the 'Bolster Stone' will be found a large hawser from which a 60ft (18m) abseil may be made down the West Ridge to gain the summit slabs of **Sgurr Dearg**.

Sgurr Dearg

From the summit of Sgurr Dearg, the broad north ridge leading to the Bealach Coire na Banachdich is one of the easiest sections on the whole traverse (W, with a short section of 1S near the bottom.) But, from the Bealach northwards, the difficulties steadily increase the whole way to Bidean Druim nan Ramh.

Sgurr na Banachdich

The long south ridge of **Sgurr na Banachdich** consists of four tops. Typically loose and unpleasant flanking paths on the L are best avoided. Easy exposed scrambling on the crest leads to the third top (actually called the 'Second Top', since they are numbered from north to south). From here, a steep descent of 100 ft (30m), called by Walter Poucher 'Sensations' (2S), leads to the last gap. Thence easy scrambling remains to the summit.

Sgurr Thormaid

Disagreeable scrambling (2S) down a loose gully on the L side of the Main Ridge leads to Bealach Thormaid, where the ridge swings to the R, and is seemingly blocked by the intimidating conical peak of **Sgurr Thormaid**. Climb directly up its steep west flank to the summit (3S). Either continue down the exposed north-east ridge, or descend well-worn slabs on the R to a faint traverse path which leads back L to the crest. The **Three Teeth** are then passed relatively easily on either side.

Sgurr a' Ghreadaidh

Ahead is the fine south-west ridge of **Sgurr a' Ghreadaidh**, described by Walter Poucher, rather exaggeratedly, as soaring 'skyward like the curving blade of a titanic scimitar.' Again, the best route keeps close to, or on, the crest (3S), while easier but much looser 'paths' may be found to the L. The 600 ft (180m) knife-edge ridge between the south and the main summits is the finest arete of its kind in the British Isles; although technically reasonable (3S), it is, in detail, intricate and totally absorbing, and there are a couple of occasions when extraordinarily exposed moves have to be made on the Coruisk side above 3,000 ft of space.

After the main summit the difficulties ease considerably. Descend an easy slope to pass an enormous nose on the ridge known as the 'Wart' on the L (west) side. Immediately beyond this, cross the ridge onto the Coruisk side and descend smoother slabs to the 'Black Notch' of Eag Dubh, which is best circumvented on the R (east) side. Regain the crest and descend to a steep wall overlooking the gully of An Dorus. Downclimb this steeply on big holds (3S) to the notch.

Sgurr a' Mhadaidh

Pull out of the notch on the north side on big, shiny holds (3S for one move), or take a slightly easier groove on the R, to reach easy ground. Continue, at first up very broken slopes, then higher quality scrambling (2S) just L of the Main Ridge to reach the summit ridge of **Sgurr a' Mhadaidh**. Avoiding an easy traverse below the crest on the L, gain the summit by crossing a fine horizontal crack in the exposed slabs on the Coruisk side. Continue down the very 'Alpine' rock crest to the point where the buttress from Sgurr Thuilm joins the Main Ridge. Here the Main Ridge turns abruptly R (to the east). Descend steep, intimidating slabs to a deep 20 ft (6m) notch at the top of the aptly-named Deep Gash Gully. Leave the notch by a stiff 3S climb and continue down further slabs to the col below the large steep step of the 'Third Top'. This is climbed well to the R (Coruisk) side (RI). Descend carefully to the even more daunting gendarme of the 'Second Top'. While this is definitely more than a scramble (RII), and on very steep, shattered rock, it is easier than it looks and very short-lived. The final ('First') top seems easy by comparison, and then a long, slabby descent on good rock (3S) leads to the welcome 'terra firma' of the Bealach na Glaic Moire (one of the few places on the Main Ridge to provide simple escape routes on either side.)

Bidean Druim nan Ramh

Immediately ahead lies the considerable obstacle of the triple-summited **Bidean Druim nan Ramh**. The first, **South-West Peak** is relatively easy (2S). An enormous cottage-sized block on the summit is bypassed on the R before easy-angled but exposed slabs are descended on the Coruisk side to the deep gap before the **Central Peak**. Zigzag , first R, then back L, on terraces; then ascend directly to the fine and relatively unfrequented summit by obvious cracks (RI).

The descent from the Central Peak to the North Peak is one of the most difficult and least obvious on the entire Main Ridge. Step down off the summit onto the very improbable-looking north ridge. Keeping strictly to the crest, scramble down carefully (3S) to a crevassed block in an exposed position above a steep step. (Various alternatives on the west side are, overall, no easier and on much inferior rock.) If an abseil is going to be made it should be done from here, and not from the badly situated slings that are usually in place about 20ft (6m) further back. It is, however, possible to climb directly down from the crevassed block for 10ft (3m), RII, to easier ground just above a narrow gap. From here, follow the crest to the exposed gap before the North Peak. A second abseil may be made from the slings that are usually in place here to the gap; or, starting about 30ft (9m) further R, one may downclimb directly on the Harta Coire side and then steeply back L down overhanging steps on sloping holds (RIII) to the gap.

From the gap, the **North Peak** is gained surprisingly easily on the Glen Brittle side, with a steep wall near the top (3S). The route down to Bealach Harta, though far less intimidating, is still not without interest. As so often on the Ridge, there is a boring, but loose and potentially quite dangerous, rubbly rake which may be followed on the Coruisk side; alternatively, by keeping to the crest, one may discover a series of easy, high-quality problems (3S–RI) on perfect gabbro. At the very bottom, the harmless-looking rake on the L (north) of the final rib leads to thoroughly unpleasant and insecure climbing on sloping holds (RI); far better is the less obvious rake on the R side which leads without difficulty (1S) to Bealach Harta (which again provides quite easy but relatively unmarked escape routes on either side).

An Caisteal

From Bealach Harta the ridge leads, with continuing interest and exposure (2S), to the fine summit of **An Caisteal**. (At one point an exciting jump is made across a deep vertical-sided notch.) From here, descend steeply L-wards on the west side to reach a short horizontal crest. A dirty gully on the R (Coruisk) side gives access to a traverse line across easy slabs which leads to a steep drop overlooking the Tairneilear Stone Shoot. An abseil here is possible, or one may downclimb carefully, at first slightly L (westwards) then back R steeply on big, but not entirely trustworthy holds (RI) to the head of the Stone Shoot.

Sgurr na Bhairnich

Climb carefully out of the Stone Shoot on easy rubbly terraces just L of the Main Ridge (1S) to regain high quality rock at the disappointing summit of **Sgurr na Bhairnich**. A long and very pleasant (1-2S) stretch of ridge now leads, with some scrambling higher up, to the summit of

Bruach na Frithe

Bruach na Frithe, but the charms of this 630ft (193m) ascent may not be appreciated this late in the day.

Sgurr a' Fionn Choire

From the summit, an easy descent (1S, W) down the east ridge leads to the small rock fortress of **Sgurr a' Fionn Choire**. Climb the crest of this directly by a short but energetic grade 2 scramble. A slightly easier 130 ft (39m) descent is then made down the L (north) side from the summit to Bealach nan Lice. It is worth noting that only another 200ft (60m) down from here, at the top of Fionn Choire, a miraculous spring may be found, which can be relied upon to provide a trickle of drinking water even in a heat wave.

The Basteir Tooth

Straight ahead lies the very intimidating axe-head pinnacle of the **Basteir Tooth**, the last major obstacle on the Main Ridge. On the Great Traverse, the only acceptable way up (despite the excellent but very indirect Collie's Route, RI, which starts way down in Lota Corrie on the R) is the classic **Naismith's Route** (RIII), which takes a superbly exposed route up the steep south-west face. From the neck of the ridge below the big frontal overhang of the Tooth make an ascending traverse R-wards above the abyss to a large ledge below an obvious crack. Care has to be taken here arranging nut belays as the big boulder which was formerly used has long since disappeared. Climb the steep wall directly above the ledge on small pockets to arrive awkwardly (crux) at the foot of the crack. Climb this for 6m, then follow another R-ward slanting crack to reach the top by a real 'sting in the tail' mantelshelf move. A short 'walk' from the belay leads up easy slabs to the summit of the Tooth. Look over the edge.

Am Basteir

Descend again to the narrow neck (actually called 'The Nick') between the Tooth and **Am Basteir**. Climb up easily round to the R (2S) then back L up a loose rake to the crest below an overhanging nose (actually, 'The Mouth'). This gives a hard and strenuous 'boulder problem' (at least RIV), but the rock is excellent and good holds are quickly reached. (An alternative way further R is only marginally easier, and on less good rock.) Scramble 70ft (20m) to the summit of Am Basteir (2S). Descend the east ridge, turning difficulties on the R (south) side. There is one short (10ft, 3m) vertical step which is surmounted by small holds on its R edge (just warrants RI), but it, too, may be avoided on the R. Further down, the temptation to follow a loose rake on the R is best resisted in favour of getting back on to the crest, which is far more pleasant.

Sgurr nan Gillean

And so to the grand finale of the whole route: the **West Ridge of Sgurr nan Gillean**. From Bealach a' Bhasteir the first step in the ridge is avoided by a path which traverses round to the L. In about 200ft (60m) a large recess is reached offering various ways up onto the crest of the ridge. The R side of the recess is now worryingly loose following the fall, in 1986, of the famous Gendarme which used to be situated on the crest. In the L side of the recess is a deep 40 ft (12m) chimney (formerly called **'Tooth Chimney'**) which is often used as an abseil route. The best ascent route is probably the steep rib to the R of this, which is furnished with good holds (RI, just). The famous **'Nicolson's Chimney'**, a slanting rake with a steep and greasy groove to start (RI), which lies some 200 ft (60m) further L, is a bit harder and definitely inferior. Above the Gendarme Shoulder, easy scrambling follows an increasingly fine crest to a final narrow arête which is gained by passing through a hole in the ridge. Excellent rock leads, fittingly, to one of the finest summits in the British Isles.

Very adventurous souls who are not by now very tired and satisfied will descend by the long and complicated **Pinnacle Ridge** (RII in this direction), or may even carry on to do the mind-bogglingly long and physically debilitating 'Greater Traverse' (over Garbh-bheinn, Clach Glas and Blaven – see next section.) Mere mortals will either reverse the West Ridge to make a rapid descent to Sligachan down Coire a' Bhasteir, or descend the south-east ridge (**Tourist Route**, 3S), in triumph. After a narrow neck is crossed, a typical 'soft option' may be found below the crest on the R but, as so often in the Cuillin, it is not much easier and leads to unpleasantly loose ground. Far better is to stick to the immaculate crest, where a vertical step is avoided by a steep groove on the L (east) side above a considerable drop (3S). Thereafter, much easier scrambling leads down to the broad shoulder between Sgurr nan Gillean and Sgurr Beag. The long walk back to Sligachan via Coire Riabhach and across the bogs I shall not describe; it is something one gets to know only too well over the years. The challenge then is to do it without getting one's boots wet.

The Winter Traverse

This is without doubt the finest winter mountaineering expedition in Britain, the most alpine in character and and yet super-Alpine in length. Unfortunately, because of its proximity to the sea, the good winter conditions that are essential are quite rare. Often when it is wintry here, ice-glazed and thus uncharacteristically slippery gabbro will be covered in a layer of unconsolidated powder snow. The standard way of doing it is from north to south, so that many of the difficult pitches can be abseiled. Because of the variability of the conditions and its length, it is difficult to give it a meaningful grade, but in good winter conditions it will be a long and serious III/IV – mostly sustained grade II, but with a number of much harder pitches and many abseils. It usually takes a minimum of two days, so that at least one bivouac will have to be prepared for (the ideal being on Sgurr na Banachdich). And even then the truth is that in all but the best conditions many will bail out after the TD Gap.

THE GREATER TRAVERSE

Traditionally the Greater Traverse, which extends the Great Traverse to include Clach Glas and Blaven, misses out Garbh-bheinn; but logically and aesthetically it should be included. It is an integral part of the Clach Glas–Blaven ridge and, like them, is absolutely at one, geologically, with the great horseshoe of the Black Cuillin.

The very strong and fit will be able to reach the summit of Blaven some 13 to 16 hours after leaving Gars-bheinn at the start of the 'Great Traverse'; but it should be emphasized that, because this extreme challenge will only be within the scope of the abnormally fit and competent, the concept of a standard 'guidebook time' is absolutely inapplicable.

The route

Sgurr nan Gillean

Sgurr na h-Uamha

Having completed the 'Great Traverse' as described above, descend the Tourist Route from the summit of Sgurr nan Gillean and continue over the minor top of **Sgurr Beag** (1S) to reach Bealach a' Ghlas-choire just north of the fine subsidiary peak of **Sgurr na h-Uamha** (which the purist will add to the itinerary by an interesting 3S scramble).

From the Bealach, descend very rough ground down An Glas-choire, keeping well L (north) of the crags of Sgurr na h-Uamha to reach, eventually, the River Sligachan. Ford this to join a faint path on the R (south-east) bank which meets up with the main Glen Sligachan path just north of the Lochan Dubha (Black Lochs). Follow this good path southwards for about 1km, then turn L and boulder hop up the stream-bed of Allt nam Fraoch-choire before striking up L to the large bealach south-east of Marsco (at the head of Coire nam Bruadaran which provides a good escape route north to the main road in 3 km). Continue due east, skirting the steep south slopes of the minor summit of Druim Eadar Da Choire to gain the fine north-west ridge of **Garbh-bheinn**. Follow this, far more enjoyably now (2S), to a well-earned breather on the summit, at least 4 hours after leaving Sgurr nan Gillean. Continue down the equally pleasant south-east ridge towards the broad bealach north of Clach Glas (1S). One short steep step may be descended directly (3S at the bottom) or avoided on the L side. Continue S for 200m across the broad, easy Bealach Choire a' Caise (which offers steep but easy escape routes on either side). At its southern end, scramble down steeper ground (1S) to gain the first rocks of the Clach Glas ridge.

Follow the long and complicated crest of the ridge southwards (2-3S), with occasional deviations on the R, towards the impressive summit tower of **Clach Glas**. Turn the last big pinnacle on the R side by an obvious traverse line to gain a broad scree gully about 50 ft (15m) below a col on the crest . Directly opposite, in the imposing final wall of Clach Glas, is an obvious chimney groove. Follow this with one or two awkward moves on its R wall (3S) to gain a small shoulder directly below the slabby headwall. Climb this directly on good holds, at first slightly L-wards, then R as the angle eases, to reach easy ground just below the superb flat-topped summit (one of the best scrambling pitches in Britain, 40m, RI).

From the far, southern end of the summit descend carefully south-east down a surprisingly easy slab just L of the crest (2S, **'The Imposter'**). At the bottom of the slab make a steep and exposed move over a small overlap formed by a basalt sill (3S) to reach easy ground on a shattered

Garbh-bheinn

Clach Glas

horizontal crest. Follow this to its end, then descend slightly R for about 50 ft (15m), ignoring a loose gully on the R, until above a vertical wall. Move sharp L (eastwards) to the Loch Slapin side, and climb down a shallow gully and then a slabby rib on its south side, in an exposed position above Choire a' Caise (R1), to reach an obvious rake which leads back R (southwards) to a notch.

After a steep pull up to leave the notch (3S), an easy but not very obvious traverse line on the L gives access to a convenient rake on the east side of the final pinnacle, and this in turn leads to the small grassy haven of the **'Putting Green'**. (An escape may be made from here down to Loch Slapin, though it is not quite the 'easy scree run' that is suggested by some guidebooks.)

Blaven

To continue the Traverse from the Putting Green, follow an easy path on the L side of the ridge for about 200 ft (60m) and then ascend easily to a small col. The short wall opposite is best climbed directly from the neck of the col on good holds, RII. (Another obvious way further L has a shelving, scree-covered finish and is situated above a more serious drop.) From here, make a long, 60m traverse R-wards across scree to reach an obvious scree funnel on the L which leads up into an impressive cul-de-sac deep in the north face of **Blaven**. A big, open corner on the R, with a chimney at its back, gives steep, enjoyable climbing on perfect gabbro. Near the top, move out R to a superb finish on excellent holds (20m, RII).

From the broad shoulder at the top of the chimney, move round blocks on the R, descending slightly, to gain a wide scree gully. Climb this for about 50 ft (15m) to the broad and bouldery **East Ridge**.

A final long slog of some 280 ft (85m) (W) now leads to the fine summit of Blaven. While this is arguably the worst climbing on the entire 14 mile Greater Traverse, it is of course, in the context, the best part of the day. To complete the Traverse properly one should continue easily south along the nearly horizontal summit ridge for 300m to the South Summit; this involves one short section of good 2S scrambling on a ledge system high up on the L (east) side of the ridge.

From the South Summit, the fastest descent to Loch Slapin takes the steep and loose **South-East Spur** to reach the broad col at the head of Fionna-choire. Then turn sharp L into Coire Uaigneich to join the path of the Normal Route which leads in 3 km to the road. If one is based at Coruisk one will be faced with the much longer descent down the superbly positioned **South Ridge** (short sections of 1S) to Camasunary; then, after fording the Abhainn Camas Fhionnairigh (guess how it's pronounced!), there is another long walk round the coastal path, passing the famous Bad Step (1S), to finally reach the stepping stones across the River Scavaig, 7 km after leaving the summit of Blaven.

A NOTE ON THE PHOTOGRAPHY

This was in many ways the most challenging photographic project I have ever undertaken, partly because of the notoriously fickle Cuillin weather, and partly because of the very strenuous difficulties that are involved when using medium format cameras in these big and demanding mountains.

The main shoot was spread over an eight month period between the end of January and the end of September 1993. A bad start, with almost continual gales and little snow, was followed by a very photogenic spring, and then an appallingly wet and dismal summer. After weeks of frustration during which almost nothing of any value was obtained, everything seemed to come right in a superbly photogenic grand finale in September. All in all, 8 trips were made to Skye giving a total of 150 days on location. The statistics will no doubt make the reader feel quite weary, and wonder how I could be so incompetent and inefficient: 64 summits in the Black Cuillin and 10 in the Red Cuillin were climbed, many several times, and 22 remote viewpoints were visited – which often involved tramping across desolate boggy moorland like a surveyor and was spectacularly unproductive considering the effort that was expended. Indeed the only satisfaction at the end of many days was simply this clocking up of heroic statistics: an absolutely genuine 191,700 feet were climbed (this is particularly easy to measure as most of the climbs start from very near sea level), 115 rolls of film shot, and 15,200 miles driven. One could perhaps express it in more revealing liquid terms e.g. so many gallons of petrol, and beer and whisky, but I think I'll keep that as classified information.

What cannot be stressed enough is that what makes a good climbing day does not necessarily make a good photographic day. Indeed, the reverse is often the case, with showery, changeable weather usually providing much more interesting light than dry but often hazy or overcast days. But the dull days are never wasted, for very useful 'recce' work can still be done (I call them 'recce photography' days as opposed to 'publishable photography' days). On very wet days with the cloud right down ('no photography' days) important research work can be done, reading books on climbing in the Cuillin, and poring over maps. One may even treat oneself occasionally to a drink at the Sligachan.

Another statistic which may be of interest – which I have found after photographing three books now in the British mountains to be a more or less unvarying constant – is that each of the three categories mentioned above will represent more or less exactly a third of the time spent on location. Thus on this 150-day shoot, there were 57 NP days, 38 RP days, and 55 PP days. (This rule of thumb only applies, of course, to a shoot which is primarily concerned with mountain landscape as opposed to climbing/action photography).

Finally, there is another 'objective danger' or hazard that needs to be borne in mind when climbing or photographing in the Cuillin. Actually, there is no way one can possibly forget about it – and I am quite proud to have got through this whole book so far without so much as mentioning it. I am referring, of course, to that infernal little beast, *Culicoides impunctatus*, otherwise known as the 'Scottish biting midge'. But perhaps it is an eloquent testimony to just how good the climbing is in the Cuillin that I haven't mentioned it; also, of course, I don't want to put people off coming to Skye and buying this book. But it is another good reason why I think that the very best times to visit are between mid-April and mid-May, and in September, when the cooler weather is anyway much more suitable for long days of strenuous hill-walking.

Photographic equipment

I have used a wider range of cameras on this assignment simply because one cannot safely take a large and heavy tripod on the more serious or strenuous scrambles. In these situations I have preferred to use one of the Fuji medium format rangefinder cameras mentioned below, usually in conjunction with the Nikon (with a very wide angle lens.)

CAMERAS
Hasselblad 500 C/M 6 x 6 cm roll film SLR camera
Fuji GW690II 6 x 9 cm roll film rangefinder camera
Fuji GS 645S 6 x 4.5 cm roll film rangefinder camera
Wista 45DX 4"x 5" field view camera
Nikon FM2 35mm SLR camera

LENSES
150mm Schneider Apo Symmar-S 150mm F5.6 (for Wista)
150mm Zeiss Sonnar CF 150mm F4 (for Hasselblad)
90mm   EBC Fujinon 90mm F3.5 (on Fuji 690)
80mm   Zeiss Planar CF 80mm F2.8
60mm   EBC Fujinon W 60mm F4 (on Fuji 645)
50mm   Zeiss Distagon CF 50mm F4
24mm   Nikkor 24mm F2.8
20mm   Nikkor 20mm F3.5
TC   Teleplus MC6 2 x Teleconvertor
x 2   Montage of two frames

FILTERS
SL   Skylight (1A or 1B) filter
UV   Ultraviolet filter
81A   Light amber filter
Grad   Graduated ND filter (2 stops)
Pol   Polarizer

FILM STOCKS
RFP   Fujichrome 50D Professional 120
RVP   Fujichrome Velvia (50 ISO) 120 or 135
RDP   Fujichrome 100D Professional 120 or 135
EPR   Ektachrome 64 Professional 120
EPX   Ektachrome 64X Professional 120 or 135
EPP   Ektachrome 100 Plus Prof 120
KR   Kodachrome 64 135

TECHNICAL PHOTOGRAPHIC NOTES

Cover	Sunrise on Blaven in the winter	9.20 am	Early Feb	Hass	150mm	f4.7	1/250	Grad	RFP
1	The Cuillin from near Elgol	5.45 pm	Late Sept	Nikon	20mm	f11	1/60	SL	RDP
2-3	The Cuillin from Sron Daraich	12.00 am	Early Mar	Wista	150mm	f27	1/15	Pol	EPP
4-5	The central Cuillin Main Ridge in winter	4.15 pm	Early Apr	Hass	80mm x 2	f9.5	1/250	SL	EPX
6-7	The Cuillin from near Drynoch	11.20 am	Late Jan	Hass	150mm	f16	1/125	None	EPX
8	Sgurr nan Gillean and Bruach na Frithe	11.10 am	Late Jan	Hass	80mm	f11	1/250	None	EPX
9	The Cuillin from Loch Harport	7.30 pm	Early Sept	Hass	150mm	f5.6	1/60	81A	RDP
10-11	The Cuillin from Tokavaig	2.35 pm	Mid-May	690	90mm	f9.5	1/250	SL	RDP
12-13	The Cuillin from Beinn Dearg Mhor, dusk	10.00 pm	Mid-May	690	90mm	f4	1 sec	SL	RDP
14-15	N end of the Ridge, across Glen Drynoch	6.00 pm	Early Mar	Hass	50mm	f4	1/15	UV	RFP
16	Main Ridge above Glen Drynoch, evening	5.15 pm	Mid-Feb	Hass	50mm	f4	1/8	UV	RVP
18	The Cuillin from Tokavaig bay	2.00 pm	Early Mar	Hass	50mm	f8	1/125	Pol	RDP
19	N end of the Ridge from Coire Riabhach	6.20 pm	Mid-Sept	645	60mm	f8	1/125	SL	RDP
21	Sgurr nan Gillean and the Bhasteir Gorge	1.30 pm	Mid-June	Hass	150mm	f6.8	1/250	81A	EPR
22	The bottom of Pinnacle Ridge in profile	5.45 pm	Mid-June	Hass	150mm	f5.6	1/250	81A	EPR
23	Sron na Ciche reflected in Loch Lagan	8.45 pm	Mid-May	Hass	150mm	f5.6	1/60	81A	RDP
25	The Great Prow of Blaven	3.15 pm	Late July	Hass	50mm	f6.8	1/250	UV	RDP
26	The Great Stone Shoot from Sgurr Dearg	6.50 pm	Mid-June	645	60mm	f8	1/250	SL	RDP
27	The head of the Great Stone Shoot	6.15 pm	Mid-Sept	645	60mm	f8	1/125	SL	RDP
28	Sgurr Eadar da Choire	9.30 pm	Mid-July	Hass	150mm	f5.6	1/125	81A	RDP
29	Harta Corrie from the top of Marsco	9.45 am	Early Apr	Hass	150mm	f4.7	1/125	Pol	RDP
31	The Bloody Stone, Harta Corrie	2.55 pm	Early May	Hass	150mm	f8	1/125	81A	RDP
31	Coire na Creiche in early March	1.00 pm	Early Mar	Hass	50mm	f11	1/125	Grad	EPX
32	Sea campion	9.30 pm	Mid-June	Hass	150mm	f6.8	1/30	81A	RDP
33	Roseroot	11.30 am	Mid-June	645	60mm	f5.6	1/60	SL	RDP
33	Ptarmigan in Coir' a' Ghrunnda	2.00 pm	Mid-June	Hass	150mm	f6.8	1/250	81A	RDP
34	Sunset on Am Basteir and the Tooth	10.05 pm	Mid-July	Hass	50mm	f4	1/125	UV	EPR
35	Upper Coire Lagan on a spring afternoon	5.55 pm	Early May	Hass	150mm	f6.8	1/500	81A	RDP
35	Sgurr Mhic Coinnich above slabs in Coire Lagan	7.45 pm	Late June	Hass	150mm	f4.7	1/125	81A	EPR
36	Peridotite boulders in Loch Coir' a' Ghrunnda	2.45 pm	Mid-Mar	Hass	150mm + TC	f16	1/4	81A	RDP
36	Oxide stains, Allt Coir' a' Mhadaidh	8.50pm	Early Mar	Hass	150mm	f6.8	1/8	81A	RDP
37	Loch lagan in May	5.15 pm	Mid-May	Hass	50mm	f4	1/60	Pol	RVP
38	Summit of Beinn Dearg Mhor, late evening	9.45 pm	Mid-May	690	90mm	f4	1/2	SL	RDP
38	Coire Lagan from Sgurr Mhic Coinnich	5.15 pm	Late Sept	Nikon	20mm	f9.5	1/60	SL	RDP
39	Rainbow and Glamaig	4.30 pm	Late Feb	Hass	150mm	f4.7	1/500	81A	RDP
40	Spindrift on Ruadh Stac	12.40pm	Late Feb	Hass	80mm	f9.5	1/500	SL	RDP
41	Loch na Creitheach, a few minutes later	12.45pm	Late Feb	Hass	80mm	f16	1/500	SL	RDP
42	Loch an Athain from the summit of Blaven	8.45 pm	Early July	Hass	150mm	f6.8	1/125	Grad	EPR
43	Cloud rolling towards Blaven	7.30pm	Mid-May	Hass	150mm	f5.6	1/250	81A	RVP
43	Wispy cloud on Druim Hain	4.15 pm	Early Feb	Hass	150mm	f5.6	1/60	81A	RDP
44	A moody morning in Coir'-uisg	8.15 am	Late Sept	Hass	80mm	f6.8	1/125	Grad	RDP
45	Gars-bheinn and Loch Coruisk	10.45 am	Late Sept	Hass	80mm	f6.8	1/250	SL	RDP
47	Clach Glas looms through the mist	4.10 pm	Early Mar	Hass	80mm	f9.5	1/250	SL	RDP
48	Clach Glas and Blaven emerge from cloud	2.00 pm	Early Mar	Hass	50mm	f13.5	1/250	UV	RDP
49	Am Basteir from Bealach a' Bhasteir	7.45 pm	Mid-June	Hass	50mm	f16	1/60	UV	EPR
50	The head of Loch Scavaig	3.20 pm	Late Sept	Hass	80mm	f11	1/125	SL	RDP
51	The author on the Bad Step to Coruisk	5.00pm	Late Sept	Hass	80mm	f22	1/30	SL	RDP
52	River Scavaig cascading into the sea	6.00 pm	Late Sept	Hass	80mm	f9.5	1/60	SL	RDP
53	Loch Coruisk at dusk	7.50 pm	Late Sept	Hass	80mm	f4	1/4	SL	RDP
54	Loch Coruisk at dawn	8.05 am	Late Sept	Hass	80mm	f8	1/60	SL	RDP
56	Spring snow, Bruach na Frithe and Am Basteir	4.15 pm	Early Apr	Hass	80mm	f9.5	1/250	SL	EPX
58/59	Sgurr Mhic Coinnich and Sgurr Alasdair, winter	2.40 pm	Early Apr	Hass	150mm x 2	f9.5	1/250	Pol	RDP

60/61	Sgurr nan Gillean in winter, from Ruadh Stac	11.30 pm	Late Feb	Hass	80mm	f8	1/500	SL	RDP
62	Snowstorm on Blaven	10.15 am	Mid-Feb	Hass	150mm + TC	f4.7	1/60	81A	RFP
63	Clach Glas and Blaven after fresh snow	10.45 pm	Late Feb	Hass	80mm	f9.5	1/500	SL	RDP
64	Gars-bheinn towers above Camasunary, winter	12.30 pm	Late Feb	Hass	150mm	f11	1/250	81A	RDP
65	Climbers on the S ridge of Blaven, February Climbers: Terry Gifford, Julian Cooper	12.50 pm	Late Feb	Hass	150mm + TC	f4.7	1/500	81A	RDP
66	Sgurr a' Ghreadaidh from Sgurr Dearg Beag	2.45 pm	Early Apr	Hass	150mm	f9.5	1/250	Pol	EPX
67	Sgurr na h-Uamha after fresh snow	3.00 pm	Early Apr	Hass	150mm	f9.5	1/250	81A	RDP
68	Bidean Druim nan Ramh from Sgurr Beag, winter	3.30 pm	Early Apr	Hass	150mm	f9.5	1/250	81A	RDP
69	Sgurr a' Fionn Choire and Am Basteir, winter	3.00 pm	Early Apr	Hass	150mm	f8	1/500	81A	RDP
70	Am Basteir etc. from Bruach na Frithe	1.25 pm	Early Mar	Hass	50mm	f13.5	1/250	UV	EPX
71	The west ridge of Bruach na Frithe	1.25 pm	Early Mar	Hass	50mm	f16	1/250	UV	EPX
72/73	The view south from Bruach na Frithe, winter	3.20 pm	Early Mar	Hass	80mm	f11	1/500	SL	RDP
74/75	The view east from Bruach na Frithe, winter	2.35 pm	Early Mar	Hass	50mm x 2	f16	1/30	Pol	RFP
76	The summit ridge of Sgurr a' Bhasteir, winter	12.40 pm	Late Jan	Hass	50mm	f11	1/250	UV	RDP
76/77	Moonrise over Sgurr a' Fionn Choire, March	4.05 pm	Early Mar	Hass	80mm	f9.5	1/250	SL	RDP
78	On the descent from Sgurr a' Fionn Choire	5.00 pm	Early Mar	Hass	50mm	f8	1/125	UV	RDP
79	The view out over distant Loch Harport	5.15 pm	Early Mar	Hass	50mm	f6.8	1/125	UV	RDP
80	Waterpipe Gully, winter	12.35 pm	Early Mar	Hass	150mm	f9.5	1/60	Pol	EPX
81	Frozen Loch Lagan and Sgurr Mhic Coinnich	5.50 pm	Early Mar	Hass	50mm	f6.8	1/15	UV	RDP
82	An Stac screes and Sgurr Dearg	7.45 pm	Mid-May	Hass	80mm	f5.6	1/250	SL	RDP
83	Loch Ghrunnda from Sgurr Sgumain	7.30 pm	Mid-May	Hass	50mm	f5.6	1/250	UV	RDP
84/85	Sron na Ciche on a winter evening	5.35 pm	Early Mar	Hass	150mm	f4.7	1/15	81A	RFP
86/87	The view west from Coire Lagan, winter	5.20 pm	Early Mar	Hass	50mm x 2	f8	1/30	UV	RFP
88	Sunset from Coire Lagan, winter	4.55 pm	Early Mar	Hass	50mm	f16	1/250	UV	RDP
89	Icy slabs at sunset, Coire Lagan, winter	6.20 pm	Early Mar	Hass	50mm	f4	1/4	UV	RDP
90	Sgurr nan Gillean in the winter	4.15 pm	Early Apr	Hass	80mm	f13.5	1/250	SL	RDP
91	On the Tourist Route, Sgurr nan Gillean Climber: John Stainforth	3.30 pm	Early Aug	Nikon	20mm	f8	1/60	SL	RVP
92	The summit ridge of Sgurr nan Gillean Climber: John Stainforth	4.00 pm	Early Aug	Nikon	20mm	f9.5	1/60	SL	RVP
93	The Dubhs Ridge rising from Loch Coruisk	10.30 am	Late Sept	Hass	80mm	f8	1/250	SL	RDP
94	Climbing the Dubhs Ridge Climber: Mike Lates	5.00 pm	Early Sept	Nikon	20mm	f11	1/60	SL	RVP
95	The top of the West Ridge, Sgurr Alasdair Climber: Neil Banks	5.30 pm	Mid-Sept	645	60mm	f11	1/125	SL	RDP
96	Starting the West Ridge of the In Pin Climber: Unknown	3.45 pm	Late Sept	Pentax	35mm	f4	1/125	SL	KR
98	A climber on summit of Clach glas	2.10 pm	Early Mar	Hass	150mm	f8	1/500	81A	RDP
100	Pinnacle Ridge, Sgurr nan Gillean	6.40 pm	Mid-June	Hass	150mm	f9.5	1/125	81A	EPR
100	Abseiling down the Third Pinnacle Climber: Dave Allan	1.15 pm	Mid-Sept	Nikon	20mm	f6.8	1/60	SL	RVP
101	The 3rd Pinnacle, seen from 4th Pinnacle Climber: Ian Banks	2.00 pm	Mid-Sept	Hass	50mm	f9.5	1/125	UV	RDP
102	Arrow Route, Sron na Ciche	4.05 pm	Early May	Hass	150mm	f5.6	1/125	81A	RDP
103	Looking up Arrow Route Climber: Mike Lates	4.00 pm	Mid-June	645	60mm	f9.5	1/125	SL	RDP
103	On Integrity, above Arrow Route Climber: Mike Lates	5.15 pm	Mid-June	645	60mm	f8	1/125	SL	RDP
104	The Cioch, Sron na Ciche	1.25 pm	Mid-Sept	Nikon	24mm	f8	1/60	SL	RVP
105	The Cioch from high in Eastern Gully	2.30 pm	Mid-Sept	645	60mm	f11	1/125	SL	RDP
106	On Sgurr na Stri above Loch Coruisk Climber: David Hope	1.30 pm	Mid-June	Hass	50mm	f8	1/125	UV	EPR
109	Final chimney, Clach Glas-Blaven traverse Climber: John Robinson	3.40 pm	Mid-Sept	645	60mm	f6.8	1/125	SL	RDP
111	Arriving on the summit of Clach Glas Climber: Arthur Ambrose	2.45 pm	Mid-Sept	645	60mm	f9.5	1/250	SL	RDP

112	The Glamaig Hill Race Runner: Pat Bonner	3.35 pm	Early July	645	60mm	f5.6	1/125	SL	RDP
113	The Glamaig Hill Race	3.40 pm	Early July	645	60mm	f5.6	1/125	SL	RDP
114	Sgurr nan Gillean, Bruach na Frithe, winter dusk	6.05 pm	Late Feb	Hass	80mm	f2.8	1/15	SL	EPX
116	Sgurr nan Gillean from Druim Hain, sunset	10.30 pm	Mid-June	Hass	80mm	f8	1/125	SL	EPR
118	Northern end of the Main Ridge, evening	9.00 pm	Mid-June	Hass	150mm	f11	1/125	Grad	RDP
120	'The Imposter', Clach Glas	5.15 pm	Late June	Hass	50mm	f9.5	1/125	UV	RDP
121	Sgurr nan Gillean from the Bhasteir Gorge	4.20 om	Late Mar	Hass	150mm	f9.5	1/125	81A	RDP
122	Nearing summit of Bidean Druim nan Ramh Climbers: Mike Lates, Bill Kemball	6.30 pm	Late Sept	Hass	50mm	f8	1/250	UV	RDP
126	High on Gars-bheinn, above Loch Scavaig	9.50 am	Early Sept	Nikon	24mm	f11	1/60	SL	RVP
127	Main Ridge at sunset, from Gars-bheinn	8.55 pm	Early Sept	Nikon	24mm	f4	1/30	SL	RVP
128	Sunrise on the summit of Gars-bheinn	6.50 am	Early Sept	Nikon	24mm	f5.6	1/30	SL	RVP
128	Leaving the summit of Gars-bheinn Climber: Mike Lates	7.00 am	Early Sept	Nikon	24mm	f8	1/60	SL	RVP
129	Loch Scavaig from Gars-bheinn, morning	7.45 am	Early Sept	690	90mm	f6.8	1/250	SL	RDP
130	Abseiling into the TD Gap Climber: Mike Lates	12.20 pm	Early May	Hass	150mm + TC	f5.6	1/250	81A	RDP
131	Climbing out of the TD Gap Climber: Bill Kemball	3.15 pm	Late Sept	Nikon	20mm	f11	1/60	SL	RDP
131	Above the TD gap with Main Ridge behind Climber: Bill Kemball	3.30 pm	Late Sept	Nikon	20mm	f13.5	1/60	SL	RDP
132/3	Sgurr Thearlaich and Sgurr Alasdair	6.00 pm	Late June	690	90mm x 2	f6.8	1/125	SL	RDP
134/5	Collie's Ledge, Sgurr Mhic Coinnich Climber: Bill Kemball	5.30 pm	Late Sept	690	90mm	f4.7	1/250	SL	RDP
136	Collie's Ledge, Sgurr Alasdair behind Climber: Dave Powell	2.30 pm	Early June	645	60mm	f9.5	1/125	SL	RDP
137	Starting up the East Ridge, In Pin Climber: Unknown	4.30 pm	Late June	Hass	80mm	f3.4	1/250	SL	EPR
138/9	The East Ridge, the Inaccessible Pinnacle	5.50 pm	Mid-June	645	60mm	f8	1/250	SL	RDP
140	Abseiling down the W Ridge of the In Pin Climber: Nick McEvett	7.00 pm	Late June	Hass	80mm	f8	1/125	SL	EPR
141	Onlookers on Sgurr Dearg	7.00 pm	Mid-June	645	60mm	f6.8	1/250	SL	RDP
142	View S from Sgurr Mhadaidh over Coruisk	7.50 pm	Mid-July	Nikon	24mm	f8	1/60	SL	RVP
142	Looking N, Sgurr Mhadaidh summit ridge	8.00 pm	Mid-July	Nikon	24mm	f9.5	1/60	SL	RVP
143	Resting on An Caisteal Climbers: Mike Lates, Bill Kemball	5.45 pm	Late Sept	Nikon	20mm	f13.5	1/60	SL	RDP
144	The Basteir Tooth from Bealach nan Lice	5.30 pm	Mid-June	Hass	50mm	f9.5	1/125	UV	EPR
144	Two people on Am Basteir	4.20 pm	Mid-June	Hass	80mm	f9.5	1/125	SL	EPR
145	Abseiling down the Basteir Tooth Climber: Bill Kemball	3.50 pm	Late Sept	Hass	150mm	f4.7	1/250	81A	RDP
146/7	On the summit of Blaven in the evening Climber: Mike Lates	6.15 pm	Early Sept	690	90mm	f9.5	1/250	SL	RDP
148	On the West Ridge of the In Pin	6.40 pm	Mid-June	Hass	150mm	f5.6	1/500	81A	RDP
149	On Bruach Na Frithe in the winter Climber: Donald Macdonald	2.10 pm	Early Mar	Hass	50mm	f16	1/250	UV	RFP
150/1	Sgurr Alasdair and Thearlaich, evening	8.15 pm	Early May	Hass	80mm	f8	1/500	SL	RDP
152	Watching the sunset from Sgurr nan Eag Climber: Mike Lates	7.15 pm	Early Sept	Nikon	24mm	f2.8	1/15	SL	RVP
153	Sgurr nan Gillean at dusk	10.30 pm	Mid-July	Hass	80mm	f2.8	1/60	SL	EPR
154	Looking towards Skye from Loch Hourn	8.15 pm	Mid-Apr	Hass	150mm	f8	1/500	81A	EPR
	The author on the summit of Clach Glas	5.30 pm	Late June	Hass	50mm	f8	1/125	UV	RDP

BIBLIOGRAPHY

Main climbing and scrambling guidebooks

DEMPSTER, ANDREW, *Classic Mountain Scrambles in Scotland* (Mainstream Publishing, 1992)
MACINNES, HAMISH, *Scottish Climbs: Volume 2* (Constable, 1971)
— *Scottish Winter Climbs* (Constable, 1982)
MACKENZIE, J.R., *Rock and Ice Climbs in Skye* (Scottish Mountaineering Club, 1982)
PARKER, J. WILSON, *Scrambles in Skye* (Cicerone Press, 1983)
SLESSER, MALCOLM, *The Island of Skye* (Scottish Mountaineering Club district guide, 1975)

Other scrambling and walking guides

BENNET, DONALD, *Scottish Mountain Climbs* (Batsford, 1979)
BULL, S.P., *Black Cuillin Ridge Scramblers' Guide* (Scottish Mountaineering Trust, 1980)
BUTTERFIELD, IRVINE, *The High Mountains of Britain and Ireland* (Diadem, 1986)
POUCHER, W.A., *The Scottish Peaks* (Constable, 1965)
STORER, RALPH, *100 Best Routes on Scottish Mountains* (David & Charles, 1987)
— *Skye: Walking, Scrambling and Exploring* (David & Charles, 1989)

Geology

BELL, B.R. & HARRIS, J.W., *An excursion guide to the Geology of the Isle of Skye* (Geological Society of Glasgow, 1986)
RICHEY, J.E., *The Tertiary Volcanic Districts of Scotland* (HMSO, 1935, 1961)

Journals

Alpine Journal —
Vol. XIII.   *The Black Coolins*, Charles Pilkington
Vol XXXII.   *The Island of Skye*, J.N.Collie
Scottish Mountaineering Club Journal —
Vol. II .   *Skye and Sgur-nan-Gillean in 1865*, Alexander Nicolson
— *The Pinnacle Route*, W.W. Naismith
Vol. IV.   *Clach Glas, Skye*, Fred W. Jackson
Vol. V.   *Early Descriptions of Skye*

General

ABRAHAM, ASHLEY P., *Rock-climbing in Skye* (London, 1908)
ABRAHAM, GEORGE D., *British Mountain Climbs* (London, 1923)
COOPER, DEREK, *Skye* (Routledge & Kegan Paul, 1970)
CRAIG, DAVID, *On the Crofters' Trail* (Jonathan Cape, 1990)
DRUMMOND, PETER, *Scottish Hill and Mountain Names* (Scottish Mountaineering Trust, 1991)
HUMBLE, B.H., *The Cuillin of Skye* (Robert Hale, 1952)
MACLEAN, SORLEY, *From Wood to Ridge* (Carcanet Press, 1989)
MACCULLOCH, J.A., *The Misty Isle of Skye* (Oliphant, 1910)
MILL, CHRISTINE, *Norman Collie* (Aberdeen University Press, 1987)
MUMMERY, A.F., *My Climbs in the Alps and Caucasus* (Oxford, 1936)
MURRAY, W.H., *Mountaineering in Scotland* (J.M. Dent, 1947)
— *Undiscovered Scotland* (J.M. Dent, 1951)
— *Scotland's Mountains* (Scottish Mountaineering Trust, 1987)
POUCHER, W.A., *The Magic of Skye* (Chapman & Hall, 1949)
PREBBLE, JOHN, *The Highland Clearances* (Secker & Warburg, 1963)
REBUFFAT, GASTON, *On Snow and Rock* (London, 1963)
STAINFORTH, GORDON, *Eyes to the Hills* (Constable, 1991)
TAYLOR, WILLIAM C., *The Snows of Yesteryear, J. Norman Collie, Mountaineer* (Toronto, 1973)
WILSON, KEN, *Classic Rock* (Granada, 1978)
— *Cold climbs* (Diadem, 1983)

ACKNOWLEDGEMENTS

As with my previous books, a great number of people have helped me in many major and minor ways. The most outstanding contribution was that of the Cuillin enthusiast, Mike Lates, who not only put up with me for many months at his home in Skye, but was a very supportive companion and never-failing volunteer for a whole range of difficult climbing/photographic projects, not all of which ended up in the book. He was also an enormous help with the highly problematic compilation of the graded list, and with the guide to the Greater Traverse. I must also make special mention of the support of my brother John and of my parents; also of my aunt, Hazel, for her ever-wonderful hospitality in Scotland.

Then there are those who have made important specialist contributions: Jeremy Ashcroft, for his superb three-dimensional map; Sandy Coghill of the Sligachan Hotel for allowing me to reproduce the pictures of Norman Collie, and of the Scottish Mountaineering Club in 1898; Margaret Ecclestone of the Alpine Club for access to a wide range of otherwise unobtainable nineteenth century journals; Nick Gent who, on his first job as a photographic assistant in the mountains in winter, had a real baptism of fire, or rather, ice; Fred Johnson of Wild Country for his skill and expertise in helping me make a large and futuristic windbreak for my camera; Sorley Maclean (and his publisher, the Carcanet Press) for allowing me to use his superb poetry, and to make one very minor amendment which will be something for the pundits to spot – also for his most interesting and helpful comments on Gaelic spellings and meanings; Eoin Macleod for his hospitality and his expert clarification of certain outlandish Gaelic pronunciations; Multiprint Laboratories, Derby, for the film processing; Bernard Newman for his geological expertise, fully aware that I have had to simplify this complicated story; and Alan Wilmot, Senior Lecturer in Biological Imaging at the University of Derby, for his rapid identification of the mountains flowers I had photographed.

Finally, for a whole range of useful contributions, and for general support, I must thank: Dave Allan, Arthur Ambrose, Ian Banks, Neil Banks, John Beatty, Kevin Borman, Ian Campbell of the Sligachan Hotel, Robin Campbell, Julian Heaton Cooper, Paul Cowley, David Craig, Steve Dean, Sandy Donald of the JMCS, Ben Douglas, Michael Fallon, Fuji film for providing most of the film stock, Terry Gifford, David Hope, Carrie Hughes, David Jones, Trefor Jones, Bill Kemball, Bob and Barbara McGovern, Ian Macleod, Malcolm Macpherson, Terry Mooney, Robin Morris of the Hill Running Commission, Michael Rhodes, Guy Richardson, Jon Rigby, John Robinson, and David Rose.

INDEX

Plates are shown in **bold** type

Abraham, Ashley, 89, 94, 103, 104, 108, 132
Allt Coir' a' Mhadaidh, **36**
Alpine Club, 91, 92
Am Basteir, **34, 49, 56, 69, 70,** 166-167
An Caisteal, 108, **143,** 166
An Garbh-choire, **44**
An Stac, **82, 134, 139,** 164
Anderson, G., 43
'Arrow Route' (Sron na Ciche), **102, 103**

'Bad Step' (Coruisk coastal path), **51,** 169
Basteir Tooth, **34,** 99, 111, 126, **144-145,** 166
Bealach Mhic Coinnich, 108, 163
Bealach Tairneilear, 108
Beinn Dearg Mhor, sunset views from, **12-13, 38**
Bhasteir Gorge, **21, 121**
Bidean Druim nan Ramh, **68,** 108, **122,** 165-166
Bla Bheinn (Blaven), **25,** 38, **43, 48, 62, 63, 65, 109, 146-147,** 169
    views from, **42, 146-7**
'Black Cuillin', 34
'Bloody Stone', 30
Borman, Kevin, 152
Brown, William, 124
Bruach na Frithe, **8, 56, 70-75, 114, 149,** 166

Caisteal a' Garbh-choire, 162
Charlie, Bonnie Prince, 30
Cioch (Sron na Ciche), **104, 105**
Clach Glas, 38, **47, 48, 63, 98,** 99, 108, 111, **120,** 168-169
Clach Glas-Blaven traverse, 91, **109, 120,** 168-169
Clearances, 30
Coir' a' Ghreadaidh, **28**
Coir' a' Ghrunnda, **33, 83**
Coire Bhasteir, 21, **100**
Coire Lagan, **23, 35-37,** 38, **84-89**
Coire na Creiche, 31
Coire Riabhach, **19**
Collie, Prof. J. Norman, 48, 94, **124,** 143
'Collie's Ledge' (Sgurr Mhic Coinnich), **135, 136**
Coir'-uisg (Coruisk), **44,** 99
    See also Loch Coruisk
Cuchulain, 124
Cuillin,
    distant views of, **1, 2-3, 6-16, 18, 19**
    geology, **20-21,** 34
    name, 19-20, 29
    Ridge, *see* Main Ridge
    weather, 46
Cuillin of Rum., 20, **38**

Druim nam Ramh, 19

Druim Hain, **43, 116**
Dubhs Ridge, 91, **93, 94**

Eastern Gully, Sron na Ciche, **105**
Elgol, **1**

Forbes, Prof. J., 91
Fionn Choire, **78, 79**

Garbh-bheinn, 168
Gars-bheinn, **45, 64, 83,** 125, **126, 128-129,** 162
Glamaig, **39**
Glamaig Hill Race, **112-113**
Glenbrittle, 125
Glen Drynoch, **6, 8, 14, 16**
'Great Prow' (Blaven), **25**
Great Stone Shoot (Sgurr Alasdair), **26-27, 59**
Greater Traverse, 168-169

Harta Corrie, **29, 30,** 68

Inaccessible Pinnacle, 96, **137-140, 148,** 164
Inglis Clark, Dr W., 100
'Integrity' (Sron na Ciche), **103**

Jackson, Fred W., 99

King, W. Wickham, **110,** 111

Loch an Athain, **42**
Loch Brittle **38**
Loch Coir' a' Ghrunnda, **36**
Loch Coruisk, **45, 53, 54-55, 93, 106, 142**
Loch Harport, **9,** 79
Loch Hourn, **154-155**
Loch Lagan, **23, 37, 38, 81**
Loch na Creitheach, **40, 41**
Loch Scavaig, **40, 41, 50, 52, 126, 129**

MacCuloch, J.A., 15
Macculoch, John, 54
MacLaren, C.A., 125
Maclean, Sorley, 1, 7, 24, 72, 115-118, 119-120, 123, 127
Main Ridge, **4-5, 12-13, 63, 72-73,** 97, 108, 111, **118, 122,** 124-127, **127-145, 149,** 162-167
    first successful traverse, 125
    winter traverse, 167
    See also Greater Traverse
mountain flora, 32
    Roseroot (*Rhodiola rosea*), **33**
    Sea Campion (*Silene maritima*), **32**
Muir, John, 50
Mummery, A.F., 99
Murray, W. H., 94

Naismith, W. W., **110,** 111
Newman, Cardinal, 91

Nicolson, Alexander, 18, 46, 119

Pennant, Thomas, 13
Pilkington brothers, 92
    Charles, 46, 139a
    Lawrence, 19, 46
Pinnacle Ridge (Sgurr nan Gillean), **22,** 91, **100-101,** 111
Ptarmigan, **33**

Raeburn, Harold, 96
Rébuffat, Gaston, 127
'Red Cuillin', 34
Ruadh Stac, views from, **40, 41, 43, 60-61**
Rum, 20, **38**

Scottish Mountaineering Club, **110,** 111
Sgurr a' Bhasteir, **76, 78, 114**
Sgurr a'Fionn Choire, 38, **56, 69, 70, 77,** 126, 166
Sgurr a' Ghreadaidh, **66, 82,** 164-165
Sgurr a'Mhadaidh, 125, **142,** 165
Sgurr an Fheadain, **80**
Sgurr Alasdair, **26, 35,** 46, **59, 95, 133, 136, 150,** 163
    See also Great Stone Shoot
Sgurr Beag, 168
    views from, **3-5, 67-69**
Sgurr Dearg, **27,** 38, **82, 137-141,** 164
Sgurr Dubh Beag, **44, 93**
Sgurr Dubh Mor, 38, **93**
Sgurr Dubh na Da Bheinn, **34,** 162
Sgurr Eadar da Choire, 19
Sgurr Mhic Coinnich, **35, 58, 81,** 111, **135,** 163-164
    view from, 38
Sgurr na Banachdich, 164
Sgurr na Bhairnich, 166
Sgurr na h-Uamha, **60, 67,** 168
Sgurr na Stri, **64, 106**
Sgurr nan Eag, **83, 152**
Sgurr nan Gillean, 8, 20, **21, 22, 61, 65, 74, 90-92, 100,** 111, **114, 116, 121,** 125, **153,** 166, 168
Sgurr Sgumain, **35, 150**
    views from, **82-83**
Sgurr Thearlaich, **59,** 108, **132, 150,** 163
Sgurr Thormaid, 164
Shadbolt, Leslie, 125
Sligachan, 21, 111, 113, 125
Solly, Godfrey, **110,** 111
Srath na Creitheach, **42**
Sron na Ciche, **23, 34, 84-85, 102-105**

TD (Thearlaich-Dubh)
    Gap, 97, 111, 124, 125, **130-131,** 163
Tokavaig, views of the Cuillin from, **2-3, 10-11, 18**

'Waterpipe Gully' (Sgurr an Fheadain), **80**
Weld, C. R., **36,** 61

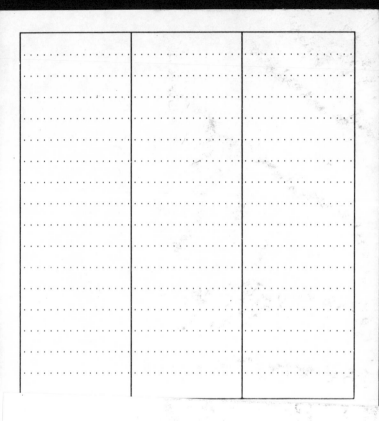